I0569046

ON RULING

AN EVERYDAY GUIDE FOR CHRISTIAN PATRIARCHS

OLD GROG

Western Front
BOOKS

Copyright © 2025 by Old Grog and the Viceroy Project
www.theViceroyProject.com

All rights reserved.

No part of this book may be reproduced in any form or by any electronic
or mechanical means, including information storage and retrieval
systems, without written permission from the author, except for the use
of brief quotations in a book review.

Except where noted, all Scripture quotations taken from the New King
James Version®. Copyright © 1982 by Thomas Nelson. Used by
permission. All rights reserved.

Western Front Books
12407 N Mopac Expy #250
Austin, TX 78758
www.WesternFrontBooks.com

ISBN: 978-1-959666-45-5 (paperback)
ISBN: 978-1-959666-46-2 (ebook)

IS THIS BOOK FOR ME?

This book might be for you and it might not be. Follow the decision pathway to find out if you're the intended audience. Maybe you know someone who would answer YES to all these questions - you could give it as a gift. But - they would probably like a steak diner and six-pack more - just sayin'.

DID GOD GIVE ME MALE REPRODUCTIVE ORGANS WHEN HE MADE ME? OR -- *YES, I HAVE A TWIG AND BERRIES.*

YES. *CONTINUE BELOW.*   **NO.** *PUT THIS BOOK DOWN.*

I HAVE GIVEN MY ALLEGIANCE TO AND SUBMIT MY LIFE TO CHRIST AS KING. I AM NOT A NEW/BABY CHRISTIAN - RATHER, I HAVE BEEN DISCIPLED/TRAINED IN THE FAITH. I HAVE BEEN IN THE CHURCH FOR A FEW YEARS NOW AND WANT MORE TRAINING, UNDERSTANDING, AND VISION FOR WHAT'S NEXT.

YES. *CONTINUE BELOW.*   **NO.** *PUT THIS BOOK DOWN.*

I HAVE, OR I AM SOON TO HAVE RATHER SERIOUS GOVERNING RESPONSIBILITIES: A WIFE, SONS AND DAUGHTERS, A ROLE IN THE LOCAL CHURCH, OR DIRECT REPORTS AT MY WORK. I WANT TO LEARN TO GOVERN MORE - I HAVE AMBITION. I WANT TO GOVERN WELL , SO THE KING GETS MORE GLORY AND GAINS MORE TERRITORY.

YES. *CONTINUE BELOW.*   **NO.** *PUT THIS BOOK DOWN.*

I CAN READ WORDS AND PARAGRAPHS AND THEN MOVE TO ACTION IF I AGREE WITH THE CONTENT. YOU'LL HAVE TO CONVINCE ME, MAN -- BUT I KNOW HOW TO CHARGE HARD AT GOOD GOALS.

YES. *THIS BOOK IS FOR YOU.*   **NO.** *PUT THIS BOOK DOWN.*

VICEROY

to:

our fathers, men who modeled faithfulness and grit and delivered most of this message to their sons by word and deed

our wives, gorgeous vines who make sweet the pains of this life and produce fruit by their words, deeds, and labors

our sons and daughters who, God willing, will see more victories and less failures than those who have gone before them

our friends, men who invite us to their campfires and aren't stingy with their scotch, wit, or ammo

our King, who deserves more glory and honor and thanksgiving-filled obedience than we will ever be able to offer

you, sir – may you, the reader, grow in wisdom, understanding, and knowledge; may the blast-radius of your life far exceed your imagination, and may all your people flourish under your governance

CONTENTS

"You may not be interested in war, but war is interested in you."

Leon Trotsky
Russian Communist Revolutionary Psycho

"...the kingdom of heaven has suffered violence, and the violent take it by force."

Christ the King
Matthew 11:12 (ESV)

PREFACE

Think about this slim book as a topographical map whereby you might find some wise coordinates to determine your headings – to find the terrain upon which you can build something like a life. That's what it offers – a few things a young-ish man might consider when striking out to build a life that expands and thrives, and brings the King the glory He deserves. This small book lands at a strange moment on the timeline – a quarter of the way through the 21st century – when so many institutions and norms are crumbling and washing out into the tides. We don't need more information – we are up to our eyeballs in information, but we don't have much in the way of understanding. And wisdom, you may have noticed, hasn't ever felt scarcer. This is the moment when we most need men who know how to govern and rule well and who have ambitions to go get more terrain. To our knowledge, this is the only book available on the topic of RULING. We haven't found another one. People think we're joking when we tell them that's our topic. They smile or spit-take, depending on the context.

So, don't think about this slim book as another 'Christian Man Book' or 'Something Something Leadership.' We don't mind telling you that we hope to never read another book on 'leadership' as long as we live. The guys who are always reading 'leadership' books are often some of the worst leaders we've ever encountered. The requirements of 'father' are so different from 'VP of R&D' or 'little league baseball coach' or 'husband.' To us, it seems strange to try and talk about 'good leadership' in ways that would relate to all these roles simultaneously. Leadership gurus act like they've been able to isolate and then extrapolate out the one variable: leadership. But leading is contextually dependent on who you're around, what's going on, and where you are placed positionally. So let's leave corporate leadership thinking in the dust as we talk about governing – about ruling. We hope by now you can tell that we're trying to put something PRACTICAL & USABLE in your hands. We're aiming at something that doesn't feel like *'low content, click-bait, write a book to grow your audience'* – something super lame like that. We're writing this as something like a baseline codex, an assembled record of 'the right now', for reference when we get to 'the whatever happens next.' We are hard-charging at the horizon, so stopping to get our papers together every once in a while seems like a good idea.

Finally, we think men, specifically Christian men, are waking up all over the globe and recognizing, as they rub the crusty bits from their eyes, that everything they love and everyone they love is under some kind of assault. They also know there isn't anyone who will do a dang thing about it; this is our moment, this is our small offering to a larger generational mobilization. Most of us got married and began raising children without a baseline understanding that it is MY job to build a civilization with a culture that is so unbelievably compelling that not only will my children want to propel it into the next millennium, but everyone who enters my orbit will be drawn to it and the King will have His increase. We have two thousand years of examples, the Scriptures, and a network of other men (Viceroys *) who mean to get aggressive and govern like maniacs so that good order can thrive, creating peace, and cultivating joy within our people and our borders. We endeavor to become Badass Warlord Chieftains (like our first father in the faith, Abraham) so our people can thrive. We have a ton of work to do, and we hope this small book helps you frame out your steps for the decades ahead.

One of our Viceroy guys has this to say: "When I began as a father, I only knew these five verses about running a home. This tiny clutch of passages was all I had in my front pocket. I hope this book helps fill in some gaps. I wish I had a framework like this twenty years ago! It would have helped a great deal." This book is trying to flush out the truths of these key passages; I hope it fits right in your hands and serves as a great guide through your next phases of life.

1-"Train up a child in the way he should go, and when he is old he will not depart from it." Proverbs 22:6

I knew I had to do some training, and it would surely serve as a foundation for a long life of obedience. There might be some wavering as a young man, but when he is old, he will stay the course.

2-"He who spares his rod hates his son, but he who loves him disciplines him promptly." Proverbs 13:24

Prompt, decisive discipline is an indication of my love for my children. That will require attention, engagement, and no delay on my part.

3-"And you, fathers, do not provoke your children to wrath, but bring them up in the training and admonition of the Lord." Ephesians 6:4

I *might* have a proclivity to frustrate my own children – overly attentive authoritarian types especially need this verse. Kids get angry and mean when they feel provoked and harshly beaten down. Again – fathers have some serious training and directing to do as unto the LORD.

4-"But as for me and my house, we will serve the Lord." Joshua 24:15

This whole circus is my circus. I answer for what happens in my 'house,' and I can make big calls. The responsibility is mine whether I do a good job, or not.

5-"Foolishness is bound up in the heart of a child; the rod of correction will drive it far from him." Proverbs 22:15

The kids are naturally foolish. In an age that exalts the purity of the young and endures all kinds of prolonged (overly sentimental) immaturity, we will be quite peculiar folks in town when we swat the silliness out of their backsides.

* Viceroy is an antiquated term for a man who governs an assigned territory for his king; he operates with royal authority and governs AS the crown in his assigned region. He's like an ambassador... an ambassador on steroids. More about Viceroys in the first chapter.

INTRODUCTION

The worst thing about a book written to, about, and from men is that it is a BOOK. We're well aware of the built-in resistance to interacting with long-form content. Heck, probably half you guys are listening to the audio right now rather than using your eyeballs. Another 40 percent won't make it to the last chapter. The remaining 10 percent will use chapter three as emergency toilet paper at the deer lease.

We get it.

We'll do what we can to keep it moving and not get us bogged down in poetry or deep multivariate research. We hope to make this stuff accessible and maybe even a 'fun' read – so far as that's possible.

We're writing this book to two audiences at once.

First, we're banging these keys for our own sons – so they have at least one more resource in their kit as they trek off to win their horizons. If they hand this to their grandsons in 50 years, we will be thrilled. *Second,* we're speaking to men who (1) know the High King assumed his coronation on a cross lauded by a jeering crowd and (2) are interested in fighting to their last breath to place a few more acres of territory under His dominion. To that end, we will speak to men across all age groups (more on that later). The men who rally around this message span various streams and expressions of the Kingdom: we're finding natural connections with devout Catholic men, Lutheran brethren, Reformed and Charismatic, Anglicans and off-the-grid house-church types. The community of Viceroy men is growing because we all feel the Spirit compelling us to step into the void – to push past the objections, and we are willing to take a few raps on the chin to advance the King's banner.

To that end, this book should feel like a user's manual, like something you'd pulled out of your glove box. This is a practitioner's guide for men in the thick of it. The Viceroy framework we're exploring aims to be of *practical* benefit. There are theological underpinnings, sure, but we think about our job in terms of loading resources into the bed of your truck to help you get on down your road. We aren't in your marriage or in your local church; we stand outside your world, but we want you to win your terrain and gain more operational control, more responsibility, and the authority that goes with that responsibility, over what our King assigns to your care.

You'll be pleased to know that a collection of great resources exists for those wishing to dig into these topics. Solid, trustworthy writers have developed the theory and architecture for what we will cover. We're indebted to such voices, and we will list as many worthwhile resources as we can after the conclusion. But this book doesn't deep dive into theology, parse the Greek, or cite historical sources. Like you, we're running through the dark, flipping pages with our flashlights and yelling at brothers to veer left at the tree line. So that's the purpose of the book. Lastly, we'll mention the two conversations that inspired this project.

Five years ago, several of us were standing toward the back of a men's conference with Styrofoam cups of very bad coffee. The main speaker at the event was Gordon Dalbey – a 'graybeard' thinker, author and leader of men. He's helped light the path for men for several decades (his resources are at the back of this book), and he's helped guide generations of men to step into their real identity. We respect him a great deal and some of us found ourselves standing next to him. One of us took the opportunity to ask a specific question: *how would you describe the current state of men in America today?*

His countenance fell instantly, and he stared into his coffee a moment before answering. *"It isn't good, and I'm not confident it is going to get any better. Ten years ago, there were thousands of men showing up to get training in how to be better husbands, dads, and leaders in their homes. Today, there might be a hundred men in a city who want that kind of training – if that."*

One of us asked him what caused such a shift.

He shot back, *"That's easy, two things. One, men get their identity, self-worth, and affirmation exclusively from their career and not their household. And two -"* At this point, Gordon began using his right index finger to swipe up and down on his open left palm. *"The smartphone came in like a tsunami wave and nobody was prepared for what that has done to our culture. But specifically, the ramifications for men and their households have been particularly dramatic. This"* – he continued to swipe – *"is easy, but households are hard."*

He sipped his coffee and walked away. We got the impression he felt deeply defeated. Perhaps he wasn't; maybe we caught him at a bad moment. But that conversation didn't feel particularly infused with optimism.

One of our Viceroy guys tells his story: A few months later, I was waiting at Whataburger for a 'to-go' order. (By the way, if you haven't tried Whataburger's spicy ketchup, prioritize it. Marvelous.) As I waited, a former high school student of mine approached to say 'hello.' I barely recognized him. Almost five years had passed since I'd seen him, but that didn't stop him from revealing his current situation. Within a minute of shaking hands, he blurted out, *"Mr.Coolasheck, I'm in a bad spot. I'm about a year out from graduating from university, but I just found out I got my girlfriend pregnant. I kinda feel responsible."*

I answered with a smile, *"Well, Jon, that's because you absolutely are responsible. It makes sense why you might be feeling that way."*

Jon returned the smile. *"Right. But see, she is Catholic, and, therefore, she intends to keep the baby."*

"Excellent news!" I answered.

"Yeah, I guess. But see, that means I might not finish my degree on time because I will have to pick up more hours at work to start taking care of my girl and this baby."

"That is probably true, Jon. I can see that. Making sacrifices for others is difficult," I added. *"But you'll make it. These people need you to be tough and endure."*

"That's not really the hardest part though," he continued. *"I don't know what a father is."*

"None of us do, when we start out, Jon. But, don't you worry..."

"No," he interrupted. *"I mean, I don't know what a father actually IS!"*

At this point, I remembered that Jon's upbringing, like that of many of my students, had not followed the traditional, established model of 'father marries mother, then they have children in a secure, enduring nuclear family.'

He continued, *"Remember that my father knocked up my mom when they were teenagers, and he split before I was born. So, no dad. Then my mother decided she was a lesbian and hooked up with my other Mom, Cindy. I was raised as an only child by two women. Neither of their dads were in the picture. So, I don't know what a father is, and I just became one."*

Someone opened the door and motioned for Jon to hurry along, so he shook my hand and fled to the waiting car. I was still putting it all together, a little stunned, when the car peeled out of the parking lot. And, in that moment, I'm almost certain I heard the King's voice say, *"Jon is the new normal. What are you prepared to do about it?"*

So – you can see that we are soon approaching the day when the term 'father' is empty. Fatherless generations will be raised by fatherless generations. Today, a well-running household – righteously ordered and teeming with joyful peace – is an anomaly. A household under Kingly order truly functions as an outpost, a frontier fortification surrounded by hostile barrenness.

In 2024, America elected J.D. Vance as Vice President; his grandmother was the singular voice of authority, direction, encouragement, and council. Without this old hillbilly grandmother, who knows where J.D.Vance might be today? Do you suppose such a young man as J.D. Vance would have benefited from a wise older man with an investor-mindset? I do. I bet there are a few young men

within your reach who would be open to some apprentic-
ing, some coffee convos, or an invitation to a firepit where
he can learn to become more than he ever imagined. This
is Viceroy work.

Suburban neighborhoods, those speckled waves of
shingled rooftops seen from overpasses, may appear to be
an orderly terrain of nurturing middle-class families. This
is not the case. Those are houses, not households. These
neighborhoods mimic the tranquility of a bygone era, but
don't buy the illusion of wonderful, thriving families.
Open marriages, third marriages, blended families, same-
sex marriages, 26-year-old men at home with mom and
second dad – our cities overflow with strange particles
colliding, combusting, occasionally reproducing,
constantly medicating, and merely hobbling along until
the next collapse.

If this were one of those 'big research' kind of books,
we could point you to a truly shocking mountain of
research that says – no, SHOUTS – that Jon's situation is
normative. But you don't need those reports. You feel it,
you see it. You might even be living it.

The dirty little secret few people willingly admit is that
the King's family now reflects what we see in the wider
culture. It's happening in the Body of Christ right now.
Our Christian families very often look like every other
family on the block.

Like Gordon Dalbey, we encounter many men trying to
stay in the fight the best they can, but they don't seem to
be 'winning' or 'expanding' – certainly not 'thriving.' We
see men stumbling under the pallor of defeat: discon-
nected from the fight they want to win, committed to
spouses by warm alliance only, and staring in confusion at

unhappy digitally tethered children with the same pity in their eyes.

Even the recent surge in 'masculinity' – the myriad of podcasts, books, elk-eating personalities, Testosterone clinics, MMA, YouTube phenoms, and bro-culture high fivers – tells me that men are grasping for something more raw, more real, more thrilling than the typical 'domestic' husband and father experience can offer. The problem with all this is that the focus is zeroed in on the 'self.' Self-actualization. Self-improvement. The truth is – men perform best when we are spent in honorable service to something higher than ourselves. Only by fighting like maniacs, laying down our lives, and pushing ourselves to the brink for the King can we enjoy the euphoria, the pulse-pounding thrill, of radical obedience. Only when we see scores of other lives transformed by our self-sacrifice – the fruitful yield on the backside of our own small deaths – can we experience true camaraderie with other men. That is the moment when men become alive and connect to their value, purpose, and meaning. The King's men are looking for a good fight - we just often don't know where one is to be found.

Tell us we're wrong. Please! We wish someone would tell us we're wrong. We'd love to hear that the King's men aren't losing ground by the hour. But we see it every day, and we receive nearly weekly reports of failing marriages and collapsing households.

It is a worthy fight, friends. A household under the King's banner, well-ordered and functioning in harmony, is a powerfully radical force on the earth. It is an act of defiance – it stands in punk-rock opposition to every spirit of this age. It is a torch – a flaming marker that the King's order is alive on the earth. It yells into the darkness: *the King has many more victories lining up in the years to come!* Between Gordon Dalbey's remarks about Christian men and Jon's tough predicament, we are further convinced that men will remain in crises unless we pursue wisdom together, develop brother-saving training, and bring our own wills into right alignment with the King.

Lastly, to those who have been fooled into linking identity, purpose, or self-worth with whatever is on your LinkedIn page, don't do it. It's flimsy stuff. Instead, we challenge you, as Dalbey recommended, to see your family in a new light. Your household bears your name, the one passed down to you, the one you steward today and send into the future with your children. If you primarily define your mission in terms of career then you can expect radical destabilization from time to time. Our families remain our families beyond all other commitments and conveniences. So let's look to the King and to our own households for our purpose. Beyond that, your work is certainly part of your life's calling, that thing you do that brings tremendous value and blessing to the earth. Embrace it. Work at it harder than your counterparts. Let your children see a man who has a full chest thumping with zeal as he works as worship to his God – but remember that your identity as a priestly, royal son stands whether you get the corner office with the great view or you have to look for new work. The King has made pronouncements about your life that stand regardless of circumstances. You might get downsized; the family farm might fail; you might have to take medical leave for treatment. The business you started with your investment capital can fail – it happens all the time, but you must go on in pursuit of your God-given destiny.

We hope one thing is becoming increasingly obvious. It's a thing we say all the time: YOU ARE THE FIGHT. Your wife and your children and the generations that follow hang on your decisions. If you keep reading and continue to ask the King for wisdom, their odds of success increase as the pages turn. Toss such realities aside in favor of the hip new sports app and odds of their success drop. We're a nation with a long history of thinking as individuals, but we see glimmers of hope that things are changing. We see men every day who are starting to wake up and think in terms of family units, multi-generational family lines, and the expansion of the King's order. Welcome to the fight. Your people need you.

You Are the Fight.

CHAPTER 1
WHAT THE HECK IS A VICEROY

ONE THOUSAND YEARS AGO, or even one hundred years ago, the contents of this book would not have made sense to anyone. *"Why would you write a book (or a pre-Guttenberg parchment) about these things?"* It would be like finding a modern text tackling such hard-hitting topics as 'How to flush toilets' or 'How to go to the grocery store and buy things you need.' This book, situated in a different time, would have been utter nonsense because there was a shared cognitive baseline concerning masculinity, households, and a man's mandate to govern his operations well. These foundational pillars – immovable, unquestioned, sure – were passed down through the centuries, providing a base upon which men built families and those families, in turn, built faith-filled communities. As a result, a prosperous flourishing flowed through generations.

You may read this book and think – *"Yeah, okay, sure. Why is this even a book? Of course."* But let us assure you that men who read this book and shrug knowingly are men of three sorts: a) they had a FANTASTIC spiritually awake father who lived these things in his rigorous daily life as well as on the big church days (Christmas/Easter); b) they come from generations of these kinds of men who worked such ideas into the soil of the family; or, c) they were raised in thriving faith communities that pulsed with spiritual life and actively pushed sons into the right spiritual, emotional, and intellectual pathways. Few men enjoy this sort of multi-generational spiritual and relational investment from their fathers. If you got this – be glad, brother – it is an enormous advantage.

A VICEROY IS

Viceroy, as a noun, often refers to a brand of cigarettes or a fancy hotel chain. The biologists and naturalists among us will know a Viceroy is also a type of butterfly. Viceroy butterflies are a smaller, almost identical species to the monarch butterfly, and this winged lesser species actually provides a clue for what we will explore in this text. Keep the image of that mini-monarch butterfly in mind as we press forward.

The term 'Viceroy' means 'vice-king.' It meant that the dignitary of a certain province spoke the functional words of a ruling crown, meaning his word was as much law as if the king had spoken it himself. This term is rarely used in the modern era of representative democracies when there is a dearth of kings on the earth. Not to mention, few functional Viceroys ever existed to begin with. A specific set of circumstances or a unique problem was required for a King to invest total power in a Viceroy. Think about it: this was a megawatt version of 'power of attorney.' It wasn't something you toss around willy-nilly. First, a Viceroy was invested with 'uber-ruling powers' (my term, go with it) only so far as a monarch could trust that man with such a weighty job. Second, a king needed a good reason to appoint a second crowned-head. A situation that exceeded the king's capabilities, reach, or vision might necessitate a Viceroy.

A great example of the appointment of a Viceroy is found in the 16th Century Habsburg Empire under Charles the 5th. You may remember from elementary school that the year 1492 was significant: the discovery of the 'new world.' You probably also remember that Spain, France, and Portugal were influential European powers interested in territorial expansion, new markets, and poking all the ground they could find with their flag poles to make sure none of those other greedy bastards took the ground out from under them. These monarchs were so interested in gaining as much territory as they could feasibly control that they established new colonies in North and South America – this necessitated the invention of something called 'New Spain.' New Spain endured for 300 years and had an outpost in Santa Fe, New Mexico. In fact, Santa Fe's founding pre-dates the Pilgrim's landing at Plymouth Rock. This is all fine and well, of course, planting royal flags in new lands is easy enough, but the governance of thousands of square miles of hostile terrain is quite a different matter.

This Santa Fe outpost story reveals an interesting truth regarding the authority and responsibility of Viceroys. The moment you claim authority or ownership over anything, you have also acquired responsibility. We do well to remember this truth. There are a thousand implications of any assumed authority-title-position. Men are often anxious to acquire power and wealth without pausing to consider the weight of responsibility. *What happens if I don't manage this well? To whom do I answer, and what are the markers of success or failure?* These are three great questions to ask at the beginning of any new endeavor. More things require more kings. We would do well to remember this as we press forward. You might consider that responsibility is a word consisting of 'response' and 'ability' – or the ability to respond. IF you have that ability, then you need to respond. But to acquire power and wealth is to have the ability to respond; it would be a dereliction of duty to *not* engage.

VICEROYS FACE WEIRD PROBLEMS

The King of Spain had a big problem. 5,225 miles separated the new territory from Madrid, Spain. And the Atlantic Ocean comprises most of that distance. The king's Viceroy would rule from Mexico City – a territory so large the Viceroy had to appoint regional governors to answer to him (after all, Santa Fe is 1,400 miles from Mexico City). Even if the king decided to make the dangerous ocean voyage, one can only imagine all the problems that might surface in the king's absence should he decide to exit Europe for a year or two to set up his realm in the deserts of New Spain. Distance was an issue.

The indigenous peoples in the region posed a few 'governance challenges,' as corporate might term it, as well. Take the northern region of New Spain. Naturally, the Pueblo Indians didn't care for their new white-skinned over-lords (uprisings, revolts, and murders happened frequently); violence wasn't the only problem. The first Catholic missionaries to the region noted that the women would approach their horses and vigorously rub their vaginas on the unsuspecting (and likely confused) animals. The 16th-century European mind could not appreciate (for good reason) that these women had sex with 'nature' in order to gain spiritual power over the creature in question. In fact, no matter what kind of press release was published, the Pueblo people had difficulty 'catching the vision' for how great life in New Spain really could be. These colliding worlds simply did not mesh, and worlds colliding is a problem for anyone trying to establish a new culture in an old terrain.

Lastly, the territory of New Spain was constantly patrolled and raided by Comanche Indians who were despised by the other indigenous people groups and posed problems for every Westerner's influence even as late as the waning years of the 19th Century. *Empire of the Summer Moon* by S.C. Gwynne is a harrowing account of Comanche raiding practices. It is a great read—we highly recommend it.

Distance and hostile locals aside, the King of Spain faced one remaining problem: who to send in his place. The King of Spain had to have tremendous trust in whichever noble he selected to rule as the king's living image in New Spain. A Viceroy, aside from risking his very life, had to give up his much-vaunted position of affluence and influence to man a forward position and bring order to a dangerously chaotic world. In fact, a full-scale war with the local Indian population (in what is today Mexico) raged on for two years. One such Viceroy chosen by the

King was Antonio De Mendoza, who rose to that challenge honoring the king's request and assuming his role, becoming the longest-ruling Viceroy of New Spain.

The great thing about being a Viceroy in Peru is that you are encountering unique problems with specific, yet completely original variables. Think about it: that Viceroy (say Mendoza) took what he knew of the Spanish crown and Spanish culture (religion, jurisdictional protocols, taxation, municipal functioning, punishment, cuisine, shipping and freight in port of call, etc.) and implemented that knowledge in the most effective way possible given completely different and novel variables. Even the King of Spain wouldn't have been able to seriously challenge his decisions, because the unique problems facing Mendoza were utterly unheard of and unable to be reproduced or second-guessed. You could easily imagine a conversation between Mendoza and the king going something like this –

"Viceroy Mendoza, I see that you increased the tax rate on palm oil over the last three years, but mining revenue is down. This is surprising and confusing. Tell me about how/why you made these adjustments."

Viceroy Mendoza would only have to give some sort of reasonable response for the king to shrug and say, *"Well, those certainly seem like workable decisions given those factors you just described. I did not know all bridges to the mining region below the falls had been flooded out the last two springs and that the mining operations were in such distress. Makes sense, I suppose. Good thinking, Mendoza."*

THE KING DELIGHTS AT EFFORT

This builds to a point. Our King – the King of kings – is so pleased when we assume our Viceroy position under His crown that we suspect He is quite forgiving of any mistakes we make in our attempts to expand His Kingdom. Why do we think this? When we see our sons *attempt* to do things as we have instructed them and *attempt* 'to push good' into any situation – when we see them struggle hard to do a thorough job and please us – our heart swells with pride. We will forgive even a totally disastrous outcome! We chalk it up to a learning experience. We are far more likely to slap them on the shoulder and say *"hey, good effort out there!"* We Viceroys should be done with misgiving about whether we have what it takes to represent our King on the earth. We will do it imperfectly. So what?! Our worst disasters are much less damaging than the absence of our presence and voice. Yet this absence is precisely the biggest problem in our thinking and our communities right now.

WE MODERN MEN HATE KINGS

A Viceroy guy tells his story: *"The Viceroy concept is difficult for modern men to grasp. First, we hate monarchs. A couple of years ago I was having lunch with a business associate in downtown Houston, Texas. As you might imagine, he was wearing cowboy boots as we had a beer. We were talking about something totally unrelated to monarchs or history, but somehow a glancing remark touched on the word 'king' and this gruff cowboy leaned forward and blurted with disgust, 'I F*# 'N HATE KINGS!' He practically roared.*

"I remember chuckling and saying, 'Hey, man, this is a big statement for a guy who hasn't ever seen, heard, or suffered under any monarchy at any time. You've never been within three thousand miles of a royal figurehead. You're a Texan in the 21st century. What's all this about?'

"He answered, 'I don't know. I just hate them. Hate the very idea. Makes me mad just thinking about it!'

"We moved on, but I thought about it later. My friend's remark is true for most of us. The funny thing is that our rebel hearts hate anything or anyone who represents unmovable authority in our lives. Though it is often unstated, we resent submission to authority. Americans are far more likely to call ourselves 'libertarians' or 'independents' or even 'anarchists' before we would self-describe as King's men."

Americans are specially groomed into this way of thinking. Here's a fun, kinda nerdy, thing one of our guys dug up. Viceroy is a French term that emerged in the 16th century and means 'vice – in place of' and 'roi – the king.' So a Viceroy stands in as the functioning king. Easy enough. The British dictionary (Oxford English) defines a Viceroy (n) as 'a ruler exercising authority in a colony on behalf of a sovereign' whereas the American dictionary (Merriam-Webster's) defines a Viceroy (n) as 'a person ruling a country, province, or colony as the deputy of a sovereign.' This is a subtle but revealing difference. From the French origin, we see a slow degradation of the very definition of the term. The French 'in the place of the King' moved slowly to the British 'a ruler exercising authority' and finally to our Yankee definition 'a person ruling.' We have diluted the power of this term century by century while exalting the identity of the common man, i.e., ourselves.

It also gives a glimpse into the boisterous cowboy in

Houston, Texas, a man so many centuries separated by time and understanding that he can hardly grasp magisterial powers. Even so, he deeply resents them.

Let us be clear, we are not advocating that the US return to our roots as colonies of Great Britain. Oh man, we are not saying that! We are emphasizing that our hearts do not like the idea of complete and total submission to authority of any sort. A king seems especially egregious because we do not vote for kings and his power remains unchecked, as well as unbalanced, by any equal branch or mechanism. We will get to this later, but you would do well to begin positioning your heart for the Return of the King (obvious *LOTR* nod) and get comfortable – desirous even – with the idea of submission. It leads to good outcomes for you and everyone connected to your operations.

A deeper dive on the meaning of submission in the appendix might help, if you are still struggling with the concept.

I'M FROM THE GOVERNMENT, AND I'M HERE TO HELP

Men today (particularly younger men) rarely know that it is their job to rule – to Viceroy their scene. (Look, we used 'Viceroy' as a verb! Try it. It's fun.) We get married, have kids, work jobs without the fundamental understanding that WE ARE HERE TO GOVERN. Because we wear a Viceroy mandate, badge, designation, title, we are here working day after day on a Viceroy Project. We're here to (literally) Viceroy the hell out of our own hearts, our households, our street, our business, our churches, and our city. Everywhere we go – every room we enter – we conduct interactions under the banner of a Kingdom. And the best part is that we don't have to worry about screwing it up! Assuming a position of authority is itself a win. Simply trying to bring good order (righteousness order) and peace and joy into a playground at a school, a testy situation waiting in line at a convenience store, or praying for a woman crying at a McDonald's table is a very Viceroy thing to do.

Young men are especially reluctant to acknowledge their Viceroy position. In an effort to diffuse a little job-performance anxiety, we tell these guys they could simply declare, "Every Thursday the __(Smith?)__ family wears green shirts!" and this would be perfectly fine. In fact, it would be the first step towards building a household culture. You could pair Green-Shirt-Thursday with a slogan about growth or **Mark 4:27-28**. Initiating is your first win! The Lord supports men who *try* to rule. We get better the more we do it. We know because we have gotten better.

Do you want proof that you will be well-supported in your effort to bring order to daily chaos? Try these two verses on for size. **II Chronicles 16:9** says, *"For the eyes of the Lord run to and fro throughout the whole earth, to give strong support to those whose heart is blameless toward him. (ESV)"* Also, **Zechariah 4:10** says, *"Do not despise these small beginnings, for the LORD rejoices to see the work begin. (NLT)"* Oh boy! What's that?! These verses encourage us to hop to it without any anxiety. Don't you dare say, "I'm just not seeing any results, and I've been working on this for a whole year!," and don't you dare entertain for a moment the lie that the King isn't noticing or supporting your efforts from both His on-site *(He is present through His*

Body) and His off-site (*He will soon return to judge the earth*) positions because He is.

THE KING'S ORDER IS

And just what sort of order do we mean to bring into our spheres of influence? Well, the King's order. We are the King's men and we represent His rule and culture. We know you are probably thinking to yourself, "I don't remember a specific nuts-and-bolts description of the King's order. Is there some sort of Magna Carta or Constitution or Mission Statement or . . . anything?!"

You're in luck. We have one passage that succinctly lays out precisely what the Kingdom of God is. **Romans 14:17-18** states, *"For the Kingdom is not eating and drinking, but righteousness and peace and joy in the Holy Spirit. For he who serves the King in these things is acceptable to God and approved by men."* So there you are. Therein lies the core basis of the entire Viceroy Project that you and I must strain and sweat to establish on the earth.

Now, we aren't going to do this by knuckling down and striving in our own ability. No sir! The fruitlessness of man's own labor is legendary, and those who build houses and guard cities in this way do so IN VAIN. **Zechariah 4:6** says, *"Not by might, nor by power, but by my Spirit, says the LORD of hosts. (ESV)"* That sounds much better than us demanding that our households and employees and young men in our fellowship snap to it! No, we won't be straining or succeeding through our own strength or wisdom or abilities, but we sure are prepared to do a little suffering. We are prepared to follow the example of our King and lay down our lives in humility for the benefit of others. We'll take some risk and we will swallow some pain as an act of worship to the King Eternal.

Back to **Romans 14:** *"The Kingdom of God is right-eousness, peace, and joy in the Holy Spirit."* The first thing that is of interest here is that most of our culture chases these virtues in reverse. Everyone is most interested in joy and deep well-being that translates to happiness. Books, podcasts, and daytime talk show hosts are obsessed with finding true joy, and they'll push any product or method-ology (no matter how screwy it is) that promises to deliver some kind of peace. The number of people who enjoy true, deep, and sustained joy and peace in the modern moment are rare, and the King's people will stand out in this respect. But notice that the leading element (and indeed, the one that ultimately secures peace and joy) is right-eousness. We cannot expect to find peace and joy apart from righteousness – not in our own hearts or living rooms or board rooms or bedrooms. Righteousness is so integral to the securing of peace and joy that the King emptied His blood to secure it for us. G.K. Chesterton has a great line: "Joy, which was the small publicity of the pagan, is the gigantic secret of the Christian." In one wonderfully succinct phrase, Chesterton highlights a profound truth: that thing which everyone pursues and blasts all over the internet (insert X, Instagram, FaceBook, SnapChat, Marco Polo, YouTube or whatever you're itching to scroll currently) is quietly being enjoyed by the King's people. The world wants the kingdom without the King – they want the fruits of righteousness, but reject the King's good order. It doesn't work like that, amigo.

CHAOS LOSES - ALL HAIL THE KING

The odd thing about righteousness is that it isn't the resting state of our cosmos. Righteousness, as a concept, is deeply related to its synonyms: uprightness, decency, integrity, order. We would argue that the threads of righteousness are not only pitifully thin and fading in our modern moment, but they have failed completely in most regards. Is our political structure well-ordered in its integrity? Our judicial system? What about our public education systems or all those rooftops that line the highways? Our economic sectors? Do we have righteous international relationships as a country? What about the marriage bed and what exactly is stored in the cookies and on our internet's history pages? What's going on in our churches across the country? Would the first-century church fathers or the Apostles, be able to join us in righteously ordered worship of our King?

It is the Viceroy's ambition to secure an orderly demonstration of the King's culture wherever we may go. But not only that – we seek an expansion of that Kingdom wherever we place our feet. There is chaos everywhere, the carnage of people's lives can't be overstated, and the destruction of families is obvious at most every turn (both inside and outside the church). The terrain where you find yourself will provide you AMPLE opportunity to bring the King's power to a myriad of problems. You were made for the destruction of chaos and the establishment of an order that does and will win. The announcement of our King's entry into the earth states it plainly in **Isaiah 9:6-7:** *"For to us a child is born, to us a son is given; and the government shall be upon his shoulder, and his name shall be called Wonderful*

Counselor, Mighty God, Everlasting Father, Prince of Peace. Of the increase of his government and of peace there will be no end, (ESV)." We run operations that establish His governance and corresponding peace in our given spaces. Hey, you there! Look out! Make way for the King!

CHAPTER 2
KINGS OUTSIDE THEIR TERRITORY

WHAT DO VICEROYS DO?

THE SIMPLE ANSWER, as you probably guessed, is: *they act like kings.* But that doesn't help us much in the early stages of the 21st century because there isn't one guy we know of who strolls around his manicured estate summoning servants by ringing bells, signing things with his signet rings and wax stamps. None of our friends issue edicts or make trade alliances with Norway for timber imports. We just don't. Most guys we know put their nose to the grindstone and have people *they* answer to. They try to squeeze 10 extra cents out of every dollar. Our friends worry about college funds and retirement and whether they'll have a job in five years. We drink the best beer we can afford, treat our wives to a fancy dinner once in a while, and keep the gutters clean. That's where our friends live. No, life doesn't feel magisterial and nobody seems to move out of our way for any reason. We don't feel like a 'king' on a Wednesday afternoon negotiating a four-way stop with three other yahoos. So, even though St. Peter said we are part of a 'royal priesthood,' we're inclined to shrug our shoulders when we contemplate what that means.

Have we been too ambitious about this whole 'Viceroy' business? Maybe we would be better served to think of ourselves as St. Paul thought about himself: as an 'ambassador' for the King. Yes, that seems better to us, perhaps? We certainly are ambassadors, listening for what the King would have us say, relaying messages, discerning insights, imparting His 'will' to others along the way. Right? That seems better. Does 'Ambassadors' feel less 'presumptuous' than claiming a 'subordinate king' status, as the Viceroy terminology suggests? Probably so.

Well, let us help connect a few dots and let's see if the 'how' might functionally match up with your 'why' in pursuit of our Viceroy mission. First, let's establish what Kings do, then we can examine how a Viceroy might pursue the same thing and lastly, we will look at examples that would work in Sheboygan, Wisconsin on Thursday morning at Harry's Diner. (Never been there, but the ratings suggest the trip is worth it.)

Let's get to it. What do Kings do? We've come up with 14 Kingly activities.

1. **GROW REVENUES**
2. **COLONIZE**
3. **FORM ALLIANCES**
4. **SHOW UP UNANNOUNCED**
5. **WAR**
6. **SECURE THE FUTURE**
7. **RULE**
8. **DEMAND RESULTS**

9. **RECEIVE GIFTS/HONOR**
10. **FEAST**
11. **APPOINT**
12. **THINK MORE THAN DO**
13. **ADJUDICATE**
14. **BESTOW THE CROWN**

Because kings do so many things (*many more than we listed here in fact*), we've chosen to break these functions up into two distinct chapters for the purpose of review. The first part will focus on what kings do OUTSIDE THEIR TERRITORIES and the second part will focus on what kings do INSIDE THEIR TERRITORIES. Chunk and chew, friends. We'll get there together.

OUTSIDE THE KINGS TERRITORY

Operational control of an environment carries real benefits. First, missteps are more easily addressed. Support structures exist – household members, trusted advisors, and even ambassadors from other nations – for kings in their territories, offering guidance and helping interpret the king's wishes throughout the realm. Think of it as home field advantage. Second, outside the king's territory a ruler must account for delicate maneuvers. Careful statesmanship is needed, and kings seek permission to enter or cross the realm of another sovereign. (This is true in peacetime, of course, a period of declared war creates different circumstances.) The big point here is that territorial markers matter, and we should always be aware of where we move and how we behave depending on our coordinates. For example, ask yourself these questions. Am I in my home or another man's home? This is a simple, but important factor worth consideration. Am I in my hometown or am I a visitor outside my city walls? Am I directed by the King into a hostile environment to establish His order? Does the King's order mean that I am to walk into a foreign environment and make a Kingdom pronouncement that will likely light a match in a powder-keg? I might *have* to do that! But I'm not going to light an accidental match if I can help it — at least not until I'm ready for the combustion.

One of the spiritual fathers around here says he often walks into a community of faith and will see something out of order. That's pretty normal. The Viceroy's job at such a moment is to quietly observe and determine the next critical step. Those decisions range from a quiet prayer to ask the King to intervene and uncover what is wrong to privately addressing or rebuking the leadership (with love and kindness, of course) or making a public remark. The Scriptures and Holy Spirit (Kingly Advisor and Counselor) are a Viceroy's only resources in such moments outside one's natural territory.

1 - KINGS GROW REVENUES

Taking spoils of war. Gleaning wealth off an advantageous trade agreement. Opening a new market. All these endeavors help support the larger efforts of the Crown. Shrewd business practices and seizing opportunities is the name of the game for the realm to grow and thrive. The more you gentlemen create, build and acquire – children, businesses, property, influence, civic responsibilities – the more you will realize that it takes serious coin to accomplish serious things on earth! We believe (and we could be wrong, of course, it's just a hunch) that the King is more pleased and more impressed with a Viceroy's performance when he has fewer resources. Let us explain. Say a young man operates on a 50K a year salary and has two kids. Let's say in one year he is somehow able to acquire a small stake in a new business, begins investing time and energy in a group of five local college kids, and acquires a new programming skill, all while keeping his lawn under control! That's pretty fantastic, we'd say. Our hats are off to you, sir!

By contrast, a man who is worth 3 million on his net worth statement but merely keeps working his job without investing in any other real enterprise or other people or doing much expanding other than what his mutual funds keep spinning off – that guy showed gains in capital. But... despite his better net gain over a year, the wealthy guy has managed a less impressive performance. That first 'poorer' gentleman in our example is being incredibly faithful with his 'one talent,' as the Gospels mention. Revenue and 'gains' are about more than money, but they are also TOTALLY ABOUT MONEY! You've got to cut a ton of hay to keep a household of teenagers fed, schooled, clothed, and rolling on wheels. Life is expensive, and Viceroys are constantly aware that we have to build money engines to keep up with the expansion and increase the King puts into our hands. Leaving the house each day, the Viceroy is poised to win exploits for the benefit of others.

This is an important point. Most men we know – maybe you know the same guys we do – would be happy to live with a fraction of the material goods and comforts their families are keen to acquire. If deer lease campsites, bachelor pads, guys' college dorm rooms, and workshops are any indication, dudes can get by with a pretty slim budget on our own. An old truck decently maintained will do the trick. Rice, beans, potatoes, tortillas, coffee, beer, and the occasional Oreo-binge suits most guys just fine. But single-dude living doesn't translate well into a functional household operation. A Viceroy guy gives a quick anecdote: *"I've spent more money on my children's teeth and vision (every one of them needed corrective lenses and braces with retainers) than I can calculate, and we're just starting to pay for their university coursework. They eat nutritious foods (with healthy portions, I might add). Heck, my dog consumes better (and more) cuisine than I'd like to provide, and he has a better health plan, too!"*

The point?! Flourishing homes, businesses, and faith communities require resources to expand. If you're looking around for who is tasked with getting those dollars, you shouldn't be. Kings go get revenues to run their territories. This is your job.

2 – KINGS COLONIZE AND SPREAD OUT

Colonialism is a dirty word right now. Today, that term is connotatively synonymous with oppression, racism, theft, and exploitation. Why would we use such a heavily laden term? I use it because the term itself, in its denotation, doesn't mean all those horrible things we associate with it. Those associative elements speak to the culture doing the colonizing. Because so many of the cultures intent on 'spreading out and taking over' were oppressive, racist, greedy and fundamentally rotten in their regard for indigenous populations, 'colonialism' as a term is utterly tarnished. The Kingdom of God and the Christian church are none of those things. In fact, the Kingdom is primarily concerned with setting men and women free, bestowing instead of taking, esteeming rather than tearing down, and empowering rather than destroying lives. That's why we use the 'c-word'. So let's look at the origins of the term and how the King means to grab more territory. Rather than using only broad brush-strokes, it's probably worth a spirited conversation over a pint to explore all the *wonderful benefits* of colonialism! We should do that someday...but let's keep moving.

When the Greeks, the first colonizers, acquired new islands or territories they did so for several reasons. First, they wanted to increase access to new raw materials and create new markets for what was produced in cities like Athens. Second, they were running out of arable land and grazing pastures, while their population kept increasing. Third, and this one seems so 'unenlightened' or 'disrespectful of indigenous cultures,' they deeply believed they had a superior culture and that they would be liberating less advanced people from their ignorance and barbarism. Shocking! The word 'barbarian' today often refers to uncivilized people or evil people and their evil deeds. In fact, that word originated in ancient Greece. Initially, it only referred to people who were from out of town or did not speak Greek, who sounded like *'barbarbarbarbar'* to the Greek ear. These uncivilized people were to be taught how to speak and use their tongues according to the norms of Greek civilization. Surely, they'd be better for it and thank their Greek colonizers, or so the thinking went.

These same factors drove colonial expansion for thousands of years, regardless of the nation pushing forward into new territory. You should know that our King too has a mind to expand – to extend His influence, to grow His numbers of sons and daughters. He means to bring MANY sons to glory. He doesn't want slaves or soldiers to conscript. He is colonizing. He is expanding and multi-plying His Kingdom because He wants sons. We have a growth mindset for the same reasons – people benefit under the King's good order. Now – we put on the mind of Christ and He made himself a servant unto His Father. We maintain a servant's mindset, but we are positionally in the royal household as sons with authority. Got that? Humble, servants' hearts as kings under the High King. Posture v. position with authority.

And our God is not a metaphorical king, you'll remem-ber. He is the literal King. He wants the literal rule over our hearts, homes, businesses, and communities. It is a worthwhile activity, by the way, to walk around your city streets and proclaim out loud: *Jesus is King over Broadview Street. Jesus is King over Detroit, Michigan.* Making declara-tions like this, with your actual breath and voice, helps to solidify in your heart that He really is on the Throne. It lets spiritual powers know where they stand and who is Viceroy on the block. You might feel silly, but these are powerful words you will be uttering. Oh, and carry along a garbage-grabber and pick-up trash as you walk like our friend Kevin does. He doesn't like the King's streets to be unnecessarily spoiled by chip bags and soda cans and Taco Bell sauce packets. He actively makes his section of town better because every bit of dominion matters. See... Kevin is a Viceroy.

3 - KINGS FORM ALLIANCES

Kings form relationships for strategic reasons: to reinforce weaknesses in a territory, to open new opportunities, to create space for shared knowledge. IF certain men know something you don't – whatever that area of knowledge or nerdery might be – you would do well to buy them coffee, lunch, or a beer. That is time and money well spent. Our family forms alliances all the time with like-hearted families. And we seek to find men who know more about all kinds of things – auto repair, financial stewardship (see recommendations after the Epilogue), good film and literature, history, scrumptious taco locations. Also, we love to ask questions. Sometimes, we even manage to ask a good one.

What might these men know and what might they be willing to share? One Viceroy drops in: *"My grandpa – an old cotton farmer who looked rather like John Wayne – used to say, 'If you'll keep your mouth shut, you'll know everything you know PLUS whatever the other guy knows.' (Ironically, he talked more than just about any man I've ever known.)"*

Alliance building can be especially potent when like-minded King's men link arms and see an opening to push something big out into the world. As an example, we ought to consider starting businesses with King's men – men who know that righteous men who *swear to their own hurt and do not change* (**Psalm 15:4)** are trustworthy. They prioritize their word and will work themselves into pain to see an endeavor succeed. It's easy to roll the dice and join up with guys like that.

A great movie reference: *Ford Vs. Ferrari* shows a picture of two men in a powerful alliance. Ken Miles tells

Shelby, "You promised me a race, not the win" when the two partnered up to beat Ferrari at Le Mans. He essentially said, "I trusted you to fight alongside me, and we hoped for the best outcome." That's the best we can hope for: a smart, tough fight for the King.

Most of the men around here have been involved in several entrepreneurial start-ups. Some have worked out well. Some haven't. Because we trusted the men in those partnership agreements, even when the agreements were fractured and we separated, we did well with one another and were able to leave the agreement in peace. Is there a better, more anti-kingdom-of-this-age kind of alliance than that? We don't think there is. One of our guys says he has one response anytime someone tells him not to get into business with friends or family: *"What am I supposed to do, go into business with enemies?"* This Viceroy makes a good point.

4 – KINGS SHOW UP – SOMETIMES WITHOUT ANNOUNCEMENT

A few instances can be seen in the Gospels where our King explicitly says, "the Lord (Master) went away and left the men with their talents . . . and many days later, the Lord returned to see his estate." This Kingly entrance is what John the Baptist alludes to when he says, *"A voice of one calling in the wilderness, 'Prepare the way for the Lord, make straight paths for Him. Every valley shall be filled in, and every mountain and hill made low. The crooked ways shall be made straight, and the rough ways smooth. And all humanity will see God's salvation.' (BSB)"* He is describing the King's approach to the House of Israel. Actual road crews prepared a king or a Roman Emperor's approach to cities so they might enjoy an easy entrance without being jostled about. John the Baptist's big announcement was to prepare Israel's heart, in repentance, to receive their King – the Messiah. This is a great invitation for our hearts and households, as well, one our hearts should be pulsing out and shouting, "Come this way! What is lacking in my life, we will raise. What parts of my life are too vaulted and proud, we will drop. Just come visit us! You can have Your way in my city!"

Two thousand years is a long time to wait for the King's return. We know. We get it. It is difficult to always be buying lamp oil as we wait for Him to show up (**Matthew 25**). But think about this: there is a little mountaintop that lies just to the east of the Temple Mount in Jerusalem called the Mount of Olives. You might remember that location from the Scriptures as the very last place on planet earth that the King touched with His feet. Remember that? He ascended (lifted off) from the planet before the eyes of His followers. They stood with mouths agape squinting into the sky. We cannot fathom that moment – can't imagine. That had to be one of the wildest things to watch, and this was before Superman or space rockets. He just lifted off the planet: nothing did that two thousand years ago. Nothing. Remember, the last thing the disciples did with the King was sing a song, and then He said, *"All authority has been given to Me in heaven and on earth. Go therefore and make disciples of all the nations, baptizing them in the name of the Father and of the Son and of the Holy Spirit, teaching them to observe all things that I have commanded you; and lo, I am with you always, even to the end of the age."* Then He 'blasted off.' The King issued His orders and left the scene. The disciples got the message:

we bring people into the Kingdom and teach them how to obey and enjoy His presence and watch for His return. Got it!

The next question they probably considered was, "'the end of the age' – that was a strange phrase, that last bit? Yes?" Surely, they thought that probably meant "I'll be right back" and it has been the happy assurance of the King's men ever since that the King's return is imminent. The wildest part – according to **Zechariah 14:1-4, 9** – is that the King will once again place his feet right where He lifted off! The King will return to the Mount of Olives. You and I don't know when, but the King is coming back. Do you suppose He is going to ask questions about what we've done in His absence? I am betting on it. The King kept telling parables about specific moments of assessment and accounting updates. The King will likely expect some results when His nail-pierced feet again touch the soil.

5 – KINGS WAR

When a King has something worth defending, He marshals the troops and lets arrows fly. Viceroys are also prepared to make radical sacrifices to see others prosper. A father who has a daughter can get rather testy when the wrong sort of fellow starts prowling around his yard, as he should. A good Viceroy who sees his wife in distress will act decisively to see she gets more support: a helper for the kids, a weekend away, or a larger grocery budget as the number of kids increases.

Kings would also war in defense of an ally. Moving on behalf of others and risking something to see a friend advance is a noble thing to do. Investing in a good man's political campaign counts. Sending a promising young man to some training seminar he's unable to afford is also a great move. In doing so, you're telling him, "I believe in you and you are a good investment." Viceroys also mimic the King when we create an offensive war to take new territory. Buying properties in distressed areas, opening nonprofits that benefit the community, pushing past resistance from those who don't care for Viceroy men (you'll quickly find them, amigo – they're everywhere) to see a new church planted... whatever it may be. Resistance is not an indicator that you've overstepped your bounds. Rather, it is more likely an indication that you are stripping away contested territory from your adversary. Wipe your brow, hydrate – then take more!

Also, one of the biggest ways you find natural support for whatever initiative you're undertaking is simply by struggling through it in real time. It *should* cost you. When your wife sees you in the fight and laying down your comfort, wishes, or precious off-hours, it makes her want to support you and your esteem grows in her eyes. Power-hungry dictators don't win the affections of their subjects or soldiers. Kings who bleed (isn't that our High King's example, by the way?) offer powerful pictures, and good hearts gravitate toward, not away from, them. We haven't always had particularly good examples of this in our homes or spiritual communities. No doubt there were big declarations made: big, sweeping visions broadcasted out to the masses. But how many men have laid their lives on the line week by week? For example, we have a friend whose father demanded to be waited on whenever he was at home with his family. He couldn't be bothered to run a vacuum or do a load of laundry. Ever. Any sort of sacrificial activity warranted a dramatic play to accentuate his suffering. He even once telephoned his wife, who was at the mall shopping for Christmas gifts with the children, and asked her to return home, where he was, to make him a sandwich. It sounds bizarre today, but these kinds of pictures explain some of the negative knee-jerk reactions people, especially young women, have to words like 'patriarchy' or 'father' or 'husband.' We should remember this and not behave as petulant children or wear a literal crown and scepter as we stomp around our houses. In short, follow the example of our King who humbled Himself and washed feet and cooked breakfast on seashores and talked with unclean people. Stay low, Viceroy. But by all means – still rule. Still govern. Still demand results. Still communicate a vision and form a 'knife-hand' – a pointer hand that directs those who need your guiding influence. Men serve well when we actively lead. That's our role and we can't shirk it. Women (and men) who hold a liberal, postmodern explanatory framework will attack you and vilify you for doing good. Just know that. You will face opposition and hostility for your faithfulness in advancing the King's interests in your scene. Your life WILL poke the bear. There will be loud screeching and sharp claws will take their swipes; if you aren't prepared for resistance or name-calling, then you should take some time and repent for your unwillingness to suffer. God gave you testicles for a reason, amigo.

6 – KINGS SECURE THE FUTURE

A king's ability to 'secure the future' simply means that a king thinks less about next week and more about distant futures. He focuses on long term goals. Kings know decisions about war or taxation or industries will ripple into the centuries that follow. Long-vision thinking is the opposite of 'hand to mouth' thinking. It asks the question: how will this impact three generations from right now? Kings think about marriages differently than most of us think about marriages, but we submit that we ought to be thinking about and in prayer about family connections and what kind of social pool we operate within. Where might our children find their spouses? It matters.

A Viceroy guy chimes in: *"My four children eventually will be interested in getting married and starting their families. Inasmuch, they will need quality, King's people with which to build their lives. Right? What are the odds of my daughters finding young men who are teenagers right now that aren't permanently wired into the internet? Will they find men who haven't spent hours equipping themselves online with wicked understandings of female anatomies and expectations? Could there be any young men out there pushed into disciplined education, young men who will know how to fight to their last drops of blood for righteousness to increase in the earth? OR is that dating pool going to be a murky cesspool of grown boys with thousands of weeds and chemicals so layered into their soil that they will be declared a 'superfund site' by the government, too contaminated for anything worthwhile to root and flourish?*

"Having taught in public education for almost a decade, I can tell you teen culture is layered through and through with all kinds of bizarre influences. They are primarily educated by the internet and the internet is toxic. Racism of all against all, narcissism, and anxiety run rampant. The most twisted forms of sex, things we never knew to imagine in our own teen years, are a click away. Things one would have had to travel to Rotterdam

to see performed twenty years ago are now available for free-viewing on your 'smartphone' – that term a sheer oxymoron.

"*Conversation number one with any soon to be son-in-law is going to be fiercely interrogative. (Remember, I love to ask questions.) 'Okay, let's cut to the chase: what have you seen, what are you 'into', and let's get very candid about what you're struggling with. Don't fudge on it, don't whitewash it, give it to me straight. You can't shock me. And if I'm going to be here to pick up the pieces from a failed marriage, I have a right to know what variables are in this equation from day one. Spill it.'*"

Viceroys must be future-oriented. If a guy moves to Minneapolis for a year to help his son's family while he finishes med-school, would that be a great use of his time resources? What are the long-term ramifications and blessings of helping the next generation flourish? That is a kingly consideration. Notice, it will cost Viceroys, and we will feel the pinch for others to flourish. But will the King be pleased? That is all that matters.

Another Viceroy drops in: "*I have one great example of this from the dentist last week. My annual teeth cleaning and scraping was accomplished by the swift and able hands of a great hygienist who is also the Kingdom-minded wife of a young man I've enjoyed getting to know as a business contact. I asked how things were going in his new venture and she said this, 'Things are going great! He loves it, and although it takes him away from the house for three days at a time a few times a month, I'm able to manage okay. I keep working and earning money as his start-up gains some lift because, thankfully, BOTH sets of our parents have moved to the area to be near us. They can work from anywhere with an internet connection, but they knew they could make a big impact on our family by helping me watch kids while my husband is traveling.'*"

Now, on the surface, this seems like they lucked out with really great grandparents, but in truth, and on many deeper levels, the implications for this family are huge. The husband has the freedom to launch into unknown waters (with limited early revenue), while the diligent and hard-working hygienist keeps making money. The kids get the benefit of many hours of spiritual and family culture inputs from the older couples, and they even help the mother as she home-schools. They run the kids through the memory work and lessons. This is one of the most epic multi-generational household long-vision moves we've encountered. These Kingdom minded grandparents are securing the future across all categories, even as it costs them certain conveniences. That young man's business is going to flourish, and, in time, it will be a revenue machine. He knows and is thankful for their investment in their generational line. Their story is inspiring. We are taking notes.

CHAPTER 3

KINGS INSIDE THEIR TERRITORIES

WHEN IT COMES to governance on the home front – in familiar territory and among your people – the Viceroy mandate to bring order to chaos remains the pre-eminent focus. Things can move from relative order to absolute pandemonium in the blink of an eye, as any father can tell you. That pink room that was once in order can degrade in a moment's notice given the properly motivated four-year-old. That household budget without proper management can be spontaneously done for. Those cars don't maintain themselves, neither do the air filters, or that 14-year-old's heart that has more emotion pumping through it than anyone could ever express despite the volume of words that are marshaled for the effort.

Houses fall apart without active management. A bunch of guys around here went on a road trip and pulled over to grab a burger. We stepped into a disgusting fast-food joint: a Wendy's in downtown Memphis – a disaster zone under no governance; we stepped over a puke pile just inside the front door. We stood in line for three minutes at Wendy's before one of us snapped to our senses, realizing: *this place is a hellhole and the food here might kill us all.* We left. Let's keep exploring this concept of active ruling a little further: how is the nation of Cuba doing? South Africa? Chaos and disorder are the resting state of most everything until mankind takes dominion. There's no doubt in my mind that the King's men bring better order than globalist villain masterminds who have their own interests in view. We start where we are, in our neighborhoods and one day, we might govern nations.

When on the home front, and with the priceless assistance of a capable, smart, and motivated wife, a Viceroy stands a reasonable chance of success. (And beautiful. She is also probably beautiful.) Be encouraged, sir. The weariness of your daily grind might be tarnishing your evaluation of your scene. Your assessment of your situation may not be accurate. Your obedience and willingness to stay in the King's fight may be going better than you think. It's always too early to tell. In some sense, it takes a lifetime for all the results to be reported. And, remember, it isn't even your assessment that matters most. The King makes the pronouncements of wins and losses. Just maneuver through your days with a thankful heart and gratitude. So here is what Kings do in their territories.

7 - KINGS RULE

Kings don't assume decisions are someone else's job. They only stop long enough to determine whether the crisis is within their domain. A king considers only one question: "Does it affect my realm, my people?" Once that is established, a king might respond: "Fine. Then this is what should happen to secure the best outcome. I will task my guy John Whitacre with this pursuit and fund whatever he needs to accomplish the plan. That's it. My realm has a need. I believe I see the problem well, so I move to action." And scene!

This sounds like a weapon's grade fantasy to most young men who are starting homes. It sounds utterly bizarre to many young men who have new wives or small children or a small sales team they lead at work. In fact, we submit that most men do NOT like the sound of this Viceroy business precisely because a unilateral action or decision has a singular point of responsibility: *the dude who made that call.* Gulp. Me?! Yes, fingers may very well point in your direction. Now, we are not suggesting that you pull your six-shooter of a mouth and start slinging lead up and down the streets of your little town, decreeing this and declaring that. Some men are a little TOO eager to start 'ruling' as they read these chapters. But, that extreme position, that over-reaction is rare today. Most of us prefer wide consultation with many counselors (not a bad thing, generally), shared decision-making with the wife (down to sweet or russet potatoes), and we are rather quick to abdicate real responsibility for truly difficult decisions regarding the management of the household. We can't tell you how often we have heard a phrase like, "That's really the wife's area of expertise," and it often references rather monumental decisions of real significance.

We're not saying you should buy a house without consulting your wife, or change jobs, or fly to Chicago without alerting the family that big home rhythm adjustments are about to transpire. That would be foolish and insensitive. But this notion of 'stepping into the void' and 'making a tough call in a critical moment' seems to cause many men to break out into a sweat. "I'll never hear the end of it if it goes badly..." or "oh, Ashley doesn't like it when I make decisions about weekend plans or budgeting" are the new normal. It takes a decisive man, a Viceroy, to make a decision that requires faith, that incurs some risk for a bold move that has a good chance of paying off. For instance, deciding not to go on the family vacation because of budgetary constraints, always an unpopular call, isn't a hill most men would die on, so we let it slide. We often take that least resistant path because "you don't know Ashley!"

Finally, Viceroys (like Kings) make sure their homes and businesses are actively looking for ways to increase blessings for others. Fostering or adopting children certainly does that. Looking out for the widow down the street, hosting neighborhood dinners, feeding the poor – all of these are ways we can train our children so they see their mission in the earth is to rule, expand the realm and stretch that banner of love to include more people.

8 – KINGS DEMAND RESULTS

Kings had a real habit of making decrees and expecting others to bend their wills to accommodate his wishes. Imagine that. Now, we should all pause to remember that much-beloved kings actually did exist in history. Not all were tyrants or monsters like King John of England, extracting every last shilling from the poor. Those kinds of kings created hero bandits, like Robin of Locksley (Robin Hood – himself a kind of Viceroy who worked subversively for the interests of the true King). You will remember that the people loved Richard the Lionhearted.

Good kings easily won the allegiance of nobles by keeping their word, understanding the needs of the populace, and leading by example. They rode into the same battles and faced the same adversaries the common archer was expected to face. They enjoyed loving devotion because they behaved as magisterial masters of their lands and people. Holding oneself and those under your roof or on your sales staff to high standards of excellence is worth establishing. This can be done without behaving like a dictator or a heavy-handed boss.

Watch this: "Team, we have these shared goals. We know the stakes and what happens if we fail to meet these markers. You've been assigned your responsibilities as I have mine. Let's get to it and convene next month to make sure we hit our marks. Ed, you let this drop off your plate last month, and we're going to need to see that exploratory report next time. You said you could do it, so I expect to see it." This sort of conversation isn't demeaning of Ed, but it does crack a whip in the room. Look alive! Rather than yelling at the son who doesn't remember to mow the yard, a stern glance across the dinner table when the yard is mentioned is often enough to let the boy know, "I did not miss the fact that the yard is unkempt. The yard is your responsibility, and this glance should be a sufficient warning." If the boy is bright and has been trained well, a raised eyebrow should be sufficient to hear a 7 AM mower roar to life the next morning.

9 – GIVE AND RECEIVE GIFTS/HONOR

The High King of Heaven bestowed gifts to His people when He gave the **Ephesians 4:8-11** ministry personnel and offices. He also receives honor from His Viceroys and from all His children. We honor the King with lives of obedience, by giving tithes and offerings, by setting aside a Sabbath's rest or seasons of prayer and fasting. We honor the King in the ceremonies and rhythms of our household, by building a Kingdom-focused culture wherever we go. We work as unto the King. We give our best efforts every hour of every day because we bear His image and His name. By the way, living like that just about solves any demands or requirements our bosses might have of us! We aren't getting written up for poor performance on our projects or KPI's because our best efforts are worship. We aren't worried about getting a boss off our back. We don't engage in inappropriate speech or interactions that require HR. We work as honor-offerings to the King. We honor the King in our internet browsing and in our purchases or budgeting.

The King is worth everything we've got! If we could give more, we would – for He is worthy of everything, absolutely everything. In time, much more of us, even our very lives, may be required. When we put knees in the dirt and pledge our lives to the King, we don't hold back bits and pieces. We don't bargain. We say, in effect, "I will walk in and promote righteousness, peace, and joy. I will extend the realm with my days and years by the Spirit's power." This is the Viceroy's mission.

It's helpful to think of ourselves as 'donor class' – we are always looking to impart, invest, and empower others in our spheres. We work hard to earn the resources to push outward to see others prosper. That's the process. The fat American consumerism mindset sucks. The investor mindset should propel us into the future.

We also look for ways to bring honor to those who deserve honor. We've made it a practice in our local church to publicly honor any older men who might attend a men's meeting (**Leviticus 19:32**). We ask them to stand, and we tell them we appreciate their presence and wisdom in the room. Americans aren't particularly good at honoring age. Nobody wins a job past the age of 40 in Silicon Valley. American society is obsessed with youth, speed, performance, and newness. Teaching people to honor age and experience is a good thing we must train back into people.

10 - KINGS FEAST

This is a fun royal privilege that every Viceroy should deploy at will. Rather than merely enlarging one's waistline, feasting allows you to bring many more people around your table. They start to enjoy the King's culture first hand and receive fellowship around a table – where they are really seen and heard and understood. The King's table begins to feel quite compelling. Isn't that what the King has done? He has brought us to His table, even when we were unworthy and wretched men with darkened understanding. And, don't forget, we feast with the King at the end of the story. There are few things more like Heaven than a well-furnished table with strangers brought near. Invite random people into your house to see your Sabbath meal, your Thanksgiving meal, your Sunday lunch. Even a coffee on the porch provides a chance to hear the story, to share the moment, that may open you both to a profound grace.

It's worth mentioning, a nice pot roast may do more to

disarm a man and allow the King access than all the printed pamphlets in the world ever could. And don't you dare worry about too much feasting with others in your home. Viceroy your budget and calendar to make room. **Luke 15** is the story the King told of the prodigal son and the older (grumpy and self-sure) son. It's a familiar story. However, we may have missed that there are three sons in the story. Our King is also a son, and He was telling the tale. He throws in a little something at the end of the story worth considering. That prodigal son in the parable gets all the attention. He is most often the focus to emphasize that the lost are able to be found. All the emphasis was on the stupid boy who suddenly woke up. Over time and with several readings, you begin to realize that the older brother was also in sad shape. The older brother thought of himself in the wrong light, not realizing that all the father owned was under his management. The older brother could have feasted or killed the fatted calf any day he liked and for whatever reason. He didn't know what truly mattered to his father – so he missed it by a mile. Sons of the Father (you and me, Viceroy!) know the mission of the family. We are heirs to the Kingdom. We should live like it and make sure our joy and our peace are as evident as our righteousness. The Kingdom is a good place to be. Get in here and have a seat at this table!

We ought to be known as festive party people. When folks think of 'religious people,' they imagine that stuffy jerk dad in the film *Dirty Dancing*. It ought not to be so. Our homes are warm, inviting incubators of joy and thanks. Those outside the King's realm are the ones bumping about in the darkness and cold loneliness of this world. Bring them in and fill their wine glass. We govern well and model faith, hope, and love well when we set the tone – when we determine to govern our hearts in such a way as to model the correct response and framing for others. One can't help but consider King Lune's good example from C.S. Lewis' *The Horse and His Boy*:

"For this is what it means to be a king: to be first in every desperate attack and last in every desperate retreat, and when there's hunger in the land ... [to] laugh louder over a scantier meal than any man in your land."

11 – KINGS APPOINT

Assigning roles and tasks is an integral part of leading anything. Who is gifted at what? *Jim would be a terrible fit for running that property - but Dave has ability and margin; he would be open to that.* When we recognize other's weaknesses and giftings, we help our family, our company, and our church succeed. More importantly, knowing our own limitations is critical. Inviting others to assist and highlighting their uniquely helpful qualifications is a tremendous benefit, one that energizes that guy down his own road. Give some autonomy. Avoid micromanaging. Offer room for them to experiment, the authority to make decisions, and the resources (power) to move the assignment along. Talk through progress markers. Dissect wins and losses and ways to improve, by all means. But pointing your finger at a guy and saying words like – *"This is a good job for YOU, Rob. Are you ready to get in there and fight for it? There are high expectations here because I know that you have what it takes."* – is a gift to a man. He might gulp and sweat today, but in ten years' time he will thank you for pushing him. Young men, specifically, are never convinced that they are equipped for the big challenges. It means quite a bit to say, "I see big potential in you, man. Here is your next move. You're going places!"

Get kids to start cutting the grass at nine years old or so. Give them cooking responsibilities. Tell them their room is their territory and you expect them to run it well. A Viceroy taps in: *"My son, a freshman in high school, is my property manager. He receives $25 a month to make sure that he keeps lawn equipment functioning, the leaves raked, and the grass cut, edged. He doesn't do all that work himself: he manages his siblings, even his cousins. He isn't on his own (I help when he requests), but this is his territory. He has a monthly checklist for what needs to happen during the 12 months of the year. I told him, 'Son, I don't want to think about it. I leave all landscaping to you – you manage it, and you will be compensated for doing so.' Sure enough, he decided that Sunday mornings, after our weekly family meeting, he'll perform a tour of the property and determine the work to accomplish that week. That was his decision. The routine he decided works best for his schedule. I'm thrilled he is tackling that.*

"My 16-year-old son manages his vehicle. He knows how to maintain fluids, tire pressure, change the oil, and rotate a tire on the Volvo station wagon. He monitors the stickers and keeps it clean(ish). I told him I don't want to think about it. His car is his appointed responsibility.

"Both are getting prepared for bigger responsibilities ahead."

12 – KINGS THINK MORE THAN DO

Another Viceroy throws in: *"I once met with the president of an oil company who described his job as making one hard decision per week – rarely more or less. He perceived his hand on the controls of an enterprise affecting many lives. He also recognized that powering a large vessel (think aircraft carrier) toward a destination means that he won't be jerking the controls back and forth. Slow, steady contemplation and measured responses are required most frequently."* You see, Kings aren't in charge of entrepreneurial start-ups or idea incubators. They rule nations. Viceroys may have to be agile in the early stages of any new enterprise – we've all been in start-up phase, but, given time and acquired mass, Viceroys may themselves spend many hours communing with the King. Households, communities, and companies often depend upon a Viceroy 'knowing the king's ways' **(Psalm 103:7).**

A Viceroy friend of ours, Steven Manuel (Abraham's Wallet podcast) is fond of saying, *"If I'm in charge of keeping my family moving along, I better become an oil refinery."* He's read **Matthew 25** – he knows that a steady supply of intimacy with the King is the only source to power his enterprises. It is wise to buy and refine oil. Viceroys keep their lamps, tanks, hands full of oil. The only way to acquire that much oil is hours and hours a week in prayerful contemplation, silence, and communion with the High King. It seems incredibly costly when we have rowdy families and demanding careers. It seems indulgent even, to set aside hours and hours during the week to build the Kingly oil reserves. Don't believe it, friend. When the tanks and reserves run dry, the gears and fittings start to fall apart: relational intimacy with the wife suffers, our kids unfairly appear to us as banshees, and our hearts lose sight of the bigger picture we hoped for. Buy and refine oil to keep your tank full and, as often as possible, siphon into others. It seems costly, but spending the time and effort and focus is wisdom.

13 – KINGS ADJUDICATE

'Adjudicate' is a fancy word for making pronouncements and declarations concerning what is good, right, and just. It may feel strange at first, but we are able to judge all things. As St. Paul said in **I Corinthians 2:15**, *"But he who is spiritual judges all things, yet he himself is rightly judged by no one."* Want to see how it might work? Good. Check it out:

- *That movie is rubbish, daughter. We aren't watching things like that.*
- *We don't use that word. It isn't part of our culture.*
- *We give to anyone who asks us for assistance on the street. That's just our family's rule: so long as I have dollars in my pocket, they are to be given to anyone who asks.*
- *We pray that pay-day-loan operations would collapse and be driven out of our city, that they would go broke and no longer be able to prey on the weak and needy in our city. When we drive past them, let's pronounce that they close down.*
- *We wear certain things, and we don't wear other things.*
- *We have rules about technology use that NOBODY else has.*

We seek to build a very specific King culture in our home. We want our decisions to honor Him, so we 'adjudicate' every day as part of our Viceroy position. We establish order in accordance with an ancient culture that is taking over. It's the culture that Noah would have known, and Abraham, St. Thomas, St. Benedict, Martin Luther,

John Knox, C.S. Lewis, and Spurgeon. It is the heavenly Kingdom we have all endeavored to represent. We enter that tradition – the tradition of those who have sworn allegiance to the King.

Sure, we will adjudicate elsewhere, as well – among employees or partnership agreements or disputes among community brothers. However, a natural progression abides in all of this: we begin by giving kingly consideration to our own hearts and homes; then, with experience establishing order in personal areas, we can move our judgments outward. The humility to address one's own eye-mote opens authority to highlight another's speck. We ought to build into our sons a drumbeat, a cadence that pulses with one thought, *"I'm the King's man. I keep an eye out for where I can invest and set things right. The King is taking over and I have a role to play."*

14 - KINGS BESTOW THE CROWN

It must be a sobering and weighty thing to wear a crown for the first time, to know it was forged centuries before and sat on the brow of other men who felt its weight. The crown, the responsibility, the honor must push so hard upon the head that it nearly buckles the knees upon first placement. (At least, it should.) Knowing the royal histories and contemplating what decisions will be made in the decades that follow are minor concerns compared to the biggest consideration: *will my progeny be trained well enough to assume the throne? No matter how well I perform my duties, they can be undone by an ill-formed monarch that follows me!* Training, educating, mentoring sons and daughters is a matter of national importance. Sir Edmund Burke called education 'the cheap defense of nations' and he is correct; the nation becomes formidable and unconquerable as our sons gain knowledge, understanding, and wisdom. That is our job. The United States faces an uncertain future regarding national defense precisely because of the societal breakdown we see in our public schools, rotting downtowns, and dysfunctional families in our suburbs.

Viceroys take the training of children far more seriously than the rest of the folks on the block. We are confident that we think about this matter more than the average citizen. The typical household sends the children off on the school bus for 12 years, hopes they get scholarships to the university of their choosing, and then wishes them well as they steer off into their own self-selected horizons. Family holidays are nice, times with grandparents are worthwhile, but, by and large, young people launch to chart their own course far too soon. Childhood and teenage years are a race to independence. But not so in the multi-generational succession of Viceroys. That is an entirely different outlook and the outlook is GOOD. The Viceroys we know increase in number, influence, and responsibility. So get connected and get crackin'.

It also means we must be constantly assessing those around us. What are their natural giftings and abilities? Who has the temperament suited to this task? Who is trustworthy? Paul told the Philippian church he was sending Timothy because he was a man who sought the interest of the King, not his own interest. In **Philippians 2:20-21**, Paul says of Timothy, *"For I have no one like-minded, who will sincerely care for your state. For all seek their own, not the things which are of Christ Jesus."* St. Paul actively looked for men who could hold the line, endure hardship, and put their own interests aside. He promoted men based on this willingness, and St. Paul was a great model to instruct aspiring Viceroys – like you and me.

The tendency is to abdicate, to take a step back and away from our responsibility in a moment, to make a hard call, to oppose a threat. We tend to want to take a side exit when a room gets hot or the stakes get high. Don't. That crown sits on your head and your people need you to make the hard calls, take the brunt of the resistance, and stand resolute. You thereby model to the rising generation what they're to be praying for in a spouse (daughters) and aspiring to be (sons). Never shift the blame. Take full responsibility for the call – for good and bad outcomes. Own mistakes and show your work – what have we learned that will power us forward and inform better decisions three years from now? Help the younger generation see your decision making process. Talk them through it. *"Dad always made the right call"* – or at least – *"we never questioned Dad's calls"* are fine sentences, but they aren't as powerful as other sentences. These are better: *"Dad trained us to think in these terms and within this framework; he said we should never trust x, y, or z – but we should be actively building a, b, and c."* This kind of thinking sets them up for their own rule and management systems. It demonstrates decision-making submitted to the High King.

CHAPTER 4

THE PLANET NEEDS MEN LIKE YOU

ON BLOOD-GURGLING PAGANS TURNED VICEROYS

IT SHOULDN'T SURPRISE YOU: most men do not believe in a cosmic order.

Let's pause – we don't mean the blood-gurgling reprobate pagans of yesteryear don't believe in a cosmic order. They did. **Psalm 16** speaks of those that *"pour out their drink offerings of blood [to other gods]. (HCSB)"* We mean the modern guy on your sales team with the perpetually shiny shoes and the old fella with the fishing stories at the barber shop and the technician you watch Monday Night Football with who serves *good* bourbon *before* the win. We're talking about *that* guy! He doesn't believe there's any need for this Viceroy business. He's not thinking about his lifespan or planet earth or even the elementary school down the block or any matter beyond himself and the immediate present. This is part of what St. Paul means when he says we were 'dead' and not 'spiritually awake' in our former lives. If you believe we are a loose connection of cells and synapses, that we're mere carbon-based lifeforms hurtling through cold dark space who cap out at 80 years or so, then you operate under a contract of purposelessness. You also possess total liberty to behave as you please. You are spiritually dead. King's men, however, do not operate this way. For this reason, our lives will seem peculiar to our colleagues and neighbors – even at Monday Night Football.

Here's an insight: darkened minds thrill at the notion of cosmic vastness, the 'unknown' and the pointlessness of it all. It quickens their pulse. A lack of boundaries and responsibilities, the absence of Truth, affords endless possibilities, options, borderless self-evolution. There is no beginning, end, or righteous governance. There sure isn't a King to whom we must answer. In breaking connection with the Cosmos Maker, we witness a surging worship of the cosmos itself so that astrophysicists and technocrats are our new priests. Lacking a true awe for a Creator, we embrace new cosmic-concurring mythologies to replace the old (i.e., *The Marvel Universe* serves as modern Olympus). We built the internet, harnessing all recorded data and information in the process. We refer to our minds as computers, and we reference how our computers 'think' and 'search' as we 'ask Google' to now remember for us. Needing gods, we have crafted them anew in our image in a multitude of ways. In doing so, we enslave ourselves to our fervor and passion.

Mankind's rebel-heart prefers chaos because randomness *appears* to afford the largest range of motion to exercise our impulses and sinful whimsy. We say 'appears' because it is a lie, of course. When men do what is right in their own eyes, they find they are immediately bound to their own lusts, tormented by the hell of their own making, and slaves to their own lies. They become husks of men, hollowed out, running about this way and that in a shell game they never know how to win. Misery follows darkness into the abyss of purposelessness and fruitless living. These men die alone either in actuality or, at least emotionally, isolated – unknown even to themselves.

We, the King's men, are spared this fate. We lift glad eyes to the heavens! Our inner parts are routinely examined by our Maker. Our souls are laid bare and exposed in deep community as we are loved well by the King and His people. All Hail the King of our hearts! This is how men were meant to live: united to the King who draws near and rescues us from ourselves. So what are we to do in response? As Viceroys, how might we funnel the thankfulness of these always renewing hearts? We can go get the men who are hostile to the Crown; teach them to be obedient to God and watch them move into their destiny.

THE KING'S COSMIC ORDER

It's been said more than a few times, by more than a few wise men, that man's chief end (our purpose and delight) is to glorify our King and enjoy Him forever. It's true. That is our purpose in the cosmic order. We must start there – at the beginning, back where we might catch a glimpse of how the King set up this cosmos in space and time. That's how we will know what kind of course we ought to chart for our lives and households.

In *The Lost World of Genesis One* by John Walton (a

really good read, by the way), Walton says that the entire cosmos really is set up to function as God's cathedral. The earth is His footstool where the King reigns. It *all* belongs to the King. Now sure, dark forces are about, cast down like lightning, humiliated, still subject to the name of the King. The Genesis chapter one account is an articulation of the ancient mind, a treatise of how our spiritual fathers would have thought about the world – it is a temple text. The earth is God's temple. We are made a little lower than the angels, the Scriptures state, and we will judge angels. Every day we walk about on a planet that groans for the revealing of the Sons of God. In **Hebrews 2** the author writes, *"for it was fitting for Him, for whom are all things and by whom are all things, in bringing many sons to glory, to make the captain of their salvation perfect through sufferings. For both He who sanctifies and those who are being sanctified are all of one, for which reason He is not ashamed to call them brethren."* Many sons being brought to glory? Glory... like high renown and honor won by achievement? Why, that sounds rather like a few men we know – a few Viceroys who help re-establish order and the King's rule on the earth! **Hebrews 2** also states – speaking of rightfully aligned men:

> *What is man that You are mindful of him,*
> *Or the son of man that You take care of him?*
> *You have made him a little lower than the*
> *angels;*
> *You have crowned him with glory and honor,*
> *And set him over the works of Your hands.*
> *You have put all things in subjection under his*
> *feet.*

Too ambitious? Outrageous? Perhaps a little too lofty for your 10-year life-goals or New Year's resolutions? But that is precisely what we know of Kingdom-minded men: they help set captives free. They bind up the broken-hearted. They nurture the earth back to health. They esteem women in their God-given roles and nature. Viceroys lead others to faith, baptize people in their back-yard pools, cast out spirits of fear and anxiety and genera-tional poverty, and pronounce blessings over children's heads. These men are magisterial in their daily gover-nance, and we're proud to know them.

Second, consider our place in the cosmic order. Our King has declared His designed order and it runs counter to the pop culture of our moment. No bother. Opposing popular culture ought not to bother us one bit. But there will be blowback. You're *going* to get some blowback. Are you ready for the rowdy business? **I Corinthians 11:2-3** says, *"Now I praise you, brethren, that you remember me in all things and keep the traditions just as I delivered them to you. But I want you to know that the head of every man is Christ, the head of woman is man, and the head of Christ is God."* Now, Viceroy, be advised: this verse will really kick over the ant-hill wherever you are. Keep your head on a swivel.

In case you missed it: the Divine order runs top to bottom starting with God, followed by our King who humbled himself and learned obedience through the things He suffered (**Hebrews 5:8**), then finally men who function as heads over households. This is a hotly contested structure as we move well into the 21st century. Such structure is why St. Paul remains divisive in many circles; yes, that St. Paul – the apostle, the martyr, the church father most responsible for most of us pagan gentiles enjoying a place at the King's table and who beckoned men away from polygamy and temple prostitutes and to loving only one wife as Christ loved the church. That St. Paul. What a scoundrel! He dared to pass on faith tenets handed down to him by the children of Abraham. But we – in our vaunted, accelerated self-illumination – split the atom and set up a WiFi router; thus, we feel permission to split the King's cosmic order whenever it isn't compatible with our post-modern sensibilities or self-defined terms.

Viceroys do not have a problem with this verse. We see it for what it is: a verse that humbles us, that causes us to review our own hearts and to scour our previous week for how we may have led our households either in obedience or disobedience. Are our people close to the King because of our governance? We embrace the radical accountability connected to this order. If it happens under our roof, it is our responsibility. Every household victory is ours to share. Every defeat and rebellion ours to grieve and set right.

VIOLENT MEN TAKE THE KINGDOM BY FORCE

Do you see how your household is part of a larger design? You put enough of these little Viceroy homes together and you have a small church – a faith community, a few more and the City of God in your city begins to expand. Little by little righteousness, peace, and joy replicate. If enough men walk their neighborhoods making large declarations about the King's intentions (He spelled out quite a few in His Scriptures), then Heaven gains more access in its invasion of our planet. The enemy of our souls loses territory.

And what kind of men are these Viceroys that they wouldn't wilt under the modern pop-assault and Twitter screeds? Unmoved. Unbothered. These are violent men who would make a wide invitation – men who declare that the King of Glory has entered their realm.

Speaking of a John the Baptist kind of preparation of our hearts, the King said a few things about John. The King said in **Matthew 11:12**, *"and from the days of John the Baptist until now the kingdom of heaven suffers violence, and the violent take it by force."* It's a good thing to build some aggression into your sons and daughters. They'll need every ounce of it. We are under assault. Right now, the Chinese government is putting the church on the rack in the East. Right now, Western universities, media moguls, corporate overlords, and tech magnates are stacking the kindling, setting center-poles, dousing the straw for the coming pyres. We operate in relative peace today, minus light harassment, but we prepare our sons and daughters to endure the pains which are the long tradition of the saints. The King has overcome the world, but his first set of 12 Viceroys paid with their lives (all but John). Violent men – ambitious men – step into their moment ready to establish the order as it has been handed down to us.

The gender wars we encounter today are both new and old. Don't let it juke you. A spirit that hates Divine Order has always been at work on the earth. That spirit opposed Old Testament prophets, and it continues to contend with every man who faces a tension and *really* wants to back down. That fight is real and requires resolve. The other bit – this upheaval about gender roles and equity among the sexes and man-spreading on subways and who gets paid what at what percentage – that stuff, while making some factual points, is 15 minutes old on the timeline. Be cautious giving it air and light to grow. It can be fruitless and erode what remaining foundational pillars have resisted the cultural rot.

Here's a great answer to anyone who wants to bark at you about your toxic masculinity. First, laugh. Laugh like a maniac. Once you've recovered yourself, ask them to point to a household in your city that has a weekly ceremony honoring the wife and mother in the home. Ask them if women are celebrated for their work and effort on behalf of the family on a weekly basis. (That's one of the reasons we celebrate Shabbat/Sabbath meals each week. It provides a space to honor the wife's labor and enter into the King's rest.) Second, ask them to point to a household in your town more dedicated to equipping daughters in education and the arts than your household. We raise tough women who know how to think and don't buy the sludge pulsing through the internet or pop culture pipelines or Instagram feeds. Tough-minded, capable, literate women who know how to care for others and patiently endure hardship are few and far between. Our daughters work in gardens and make pottery, play instruments and can pass Calculus exams. They'll go toe to toe with anyone, but they also know how to respond to authority and know when to hold their tongue, just like our sons. The most toxic of all masculinity is found in the world we actively topple. The King's culture didn't invent the Dallas Cowboys cheerleaders. We didn't advance the foundational footings of Las Vegas or internet porn or create conditions where daughters are abandoned or left to poverty or left to decay in the back of badly run schools. That isn't how our King builds people, daughters or sons.

We don't allow our boys to speak ill of women, to objectify their bodies or humiliate their contributions to our households, or think they are superior to their sisters. We want tough daughters and thoughtful sons trained for war in a world that hates them and needs them. Viceroy families honor every part, but we know the sexes have different assignments, roles, giftings and tendencies as God made them.

So, once all that is established, ask them to clarify the complaint about your toxic masculinity. Or, better yet, invite them to dinner, serve them a nice brisket. Let them see your home function under the King's banner. The masses roar and convulse, but it's their rebellion to the King that has them in their own frothy-mouthed fits.

BLOWBACK

The Viceroys we know often say that it feels like we are 'farming in no-man's-land,' laboring daily with the rising sun. We wipe noses and butts and pour Cheerios and repair alternators on Chevrolet Suburbans. We plant seeds, offer desperate prayers at hospital bedsides, discipline kids, and pay our tithes. At the same time, amid all this labor, we are taking FIRE! A mounting hostility is becoming unmistakable. We face an aggressive firing line when we say the old truths, when we hold the line and don't sway in the changing winds.

Guys remind us that there is a mounting pressure to be always tethered, always in-the-know – always informed and outfitted with an opinion on just about everything. FOMO is real. Who has the hot-take on the thrilling issue of the moment? How will I get through the next batch of

MEMES? We feel a compulsion to stay abreast of whatever is happening *right now*, pulling our six-shooter and firing away, retweeting ourselves silly. Our national sport isn't baseball, as is popularly conceived. Our national sport is Democrat and Republican politics: it's the Reds versus the Blues, and a new World Series happens every four years. A steady diet of this stuff leads to rising heart rates and the wringing of hands, along with severe vilification of the opponent.

The King's men sniffed all this out a long time ago. We know this social media madness is spiritual, emotional, creative quicksand, and in it we can churn ourselves to an exhausted digital death. Viceroys don't behave this way. We don't log hours in this sort of madness. There is too much to do, too many lives to touch, too much to invest in that doesn't evaporate with the next headline. The spirit of this age (the zeitgeist) opposes our efforts, but we are increasingly adept at counter-attacks and farming faithfulness (Psalm 37:3 – dwell in the land and cultivate faithfulness) as the mortars fly overhead. Won't it surprise everyone when the fruiting bursts forth and the harvesting baskets overflow?! Fighting in quiet faithfulness must truly perplex our enemy. And when we rejoice in the midst of suffering, well, it must drive him bananas. The King is worth celebrating and quiet lives are loud declarations of worship. We fight like maniacs as we run an orderly third period classroom, when we sell roof shingles with integrity, when we don't lie to our advantage, when we unclench our knuckles from the steering wheel in maddening traffic, when we close the computer at the first sign of weariness or weakness rather than look at pornography, when we run our department with eyes to see our team flourish and gain life-changing skills under our care. All this mundane, quiet obedience is itself a vein-popping throat-roar of a battle cry that the King is marching, the Viceroys are on the scene, and our victory was assured on the first Easter Sunday when the King was glorified. That ain't a bad way to take the field.

CHAPTER 5
IT'S YOU, AMIGO – YOU ARE THE FIGHT

SELF

MOMENTS WILL OCCUR in your life – perhaps you've already encountered them – when the easiest option, the one that means the least amount of pain, will be so tempting that you'll consider bugging out. Just for a second. You will blink and consider playing dead or slouching away or just freaking out and buying a plane ticket to Bogota, Colombia. You might even be tempted to do an about-face and lead a charge against your brothers and our King! The pressures will mount, and the stakes will feel too high, and all the eyes will be on you. At that moment, you're going to have to make the call. *Do I take that job in Baltimore that pays less but I believe in what they're building – is this where we're to build our lives and root into a specific community? How do we both homeschool the kids and live on one salary with the property taxes around here?* You may be falsely accused of the worst kind of motives. You may even have only partial support from your wife or your community. They might make you take the fall, jam a mic in your face for comment, or force you to take the stand. Pressure. In those moments, you'll have to choose against your own interests. And let's be candid here: our culture isn't good about training us to lay down our lives for others. Thankfully, we have a King who excels at it.

A Viceroy bro chimes in: *"I had a great uncle named Willy. He was never formally educated, and he worked a pretty mediocre job with a barely sufficient salary and no real acclaim. He married a woman who, late in life and after a long illness, developed an addiction to pain medications. She got busted forging a prescription and served a brief stint in a women's prison. My great uncle endured it all with this messed-up wife and stood by her like a granite pillar. He raised the four boys, fixed their lunch-sacks in the mornings, coached their ball games, did the house cleaning while his wife went through detox and incarceration. He suffered humiliation as people on the block wagged their tongues. As a quiet, principled man, he did not divorce her. He didn't check out and start drinking. He held the line. I remember the car ride when my mother told me, as a young boy at the time, the whole story. She ended the story by saying, 'Your uncle Willy is the kind of man you should try to become. He didn't get shook. He persevered because he knew he was the only chance those boys had for an almost-normal life. I'm proud of him.'"*

My point is that *men leave their wives for much less than this today.* And vice-versa; we know that ⅔ of divorces are initiated by the wife. We are told, even from church pulpits, that your self-actualization is the preeminent consideration of your life. We aren't tutored into choosing pain or taking stands that chip away at our street cred or acclaim. We aren't taught to take the low road of self-sacrifice, but this is the greatest terrain you'll ever stake out for the King. Your own heart is ground zero for almost every skirmish, and you won't be able to determine what is happening in the deepest reaches and dungeons of that mysterious terrain. You're going to have to be constantly submitting your life for the King's review. You can daily ask the King to make His examination of your heart and mind. Ask Him to survey and highlight the swamplands that need to be drained, the dark coves and crags that hide the disease of self-sufficiency and that exalt our own wills above the King's claims to ALL OF IT.

We aren't going to make real progress in our homes, with our wives and children and grandchildren, until we know how to bring our own hearts under Kingly rule. Our hearts will resist radical obedience at every turn. We aren't going to be effective in our faith communities or in bringing co-workers into the King's realm until we know how to bend our knees and drop the neck whenever the King points to some area in need of submission. The battle for all is the battle for this rebellious heart. That's why we Viceroys often remind each other: YOU ARE THE FIGHT.

Americans worship mirrors (remember how we make our gods into our own image), and our icons look too much like us. We worship the Self because we have rebel hearts and because we have 'orphan thinking.' An orphan must fight for every bite of food. He is his own provisioner and his own protection. The preservation of the Self is the orphan's preeminent concern. But you and I have a Father. We are royal sons, although some of us are not entirely convinced of it. We don't yet know who we are or that we are of the Household of Faith or that the King's plans are much better than our own. Money, sex, and power – the unholy trinity of our culture – woo us into their temple, and, because that temple is so ubiquitous in America, we're barely conscious we stand so close to its altar. Let's see how all this works out.

BODY

Let's start with our appetites. St. Paul drew strong parallels with our food appetite and our sex appetite. They are linked in **I Corinthians 6:12-14,** *"All things are lawful for me, but all things are not helpful. All things are lawful for me, but I will not be brought under the power of any. Foods for the stomach and the stomach for foods, but God will destroy both it and them. Now the body is not for sexual immorality but for the Lord, and the Lord for the body. And God both raised up the Lord and will also raise us up by His power."* The reason Paul mentions this linking between sex and food is that Roman culture linked the two: orgies and feasting were normal parts of any pagan worship. Americans may have invented Hooters, but there really isn't anything new under the sun. The gut and reproductive organs are big forces in any man's life, and simply giving in to whatever appetite shouts the loudest, at any given moment, is not a life of Kingly worship. Those Romans thought about it like this: *"My belly wants food, so I give it food. My body wants sex, so I give it sex."* But St. Paul says quite clearly to those Romans, *"Offer your bodies as a living sacrifice (NIV)"* (**Romans 12:1**). You are under command, and, as such, you can bring your body into alignment with the King's orders. So stand up straight and answer in the affirmative that your body, your belly or your loins, is not the king of your life.

I should stop here and say there are VERY few men I

know who have their appetites under Kingly control. Life here in the New Roaring '20s is all about servicing our appetites. Drivers show up in delivery service cars carrying our high-end Thai-infusion tacos at the click of an app. Other drivers can haul us home discreetly after desecrating ourselves with all manner of celebratory or medicinal beverages. We can purchase any guilty pleasure online, hiding the receipt and the package, without needing to look a sales clerk in the eye. We can connect with old flames and kindle our hearts in wayward directions via hidden windows and carefully labeled files. We can lock the doors, close the blinds, and endlessly binge ourselves into zombified states of bug-eyed entertainment with our 'comfort food' for an entire weekend with no concern for being labeled 'slothful.' We can access images of women and men (and more!) doing just about anything with anyone in no time, and then we can make the evidence disappear. This has never been true anywhere at any time, but it is true today.

Sexual appetites in say 1700 were only satisfied by your wife or by the very public act of visiting the seedy part of town – walking specific dark streets – and paying for your infidelity with coins. Magazines came along, but, even then, a man had to look somebody in the eyes and pay for his purchase at a convenience store. Cable charges and hotel room bills still had a human/transaction cost. That's no longer the case. Total anonymity and total roaming through the darkest appetites are accessible via a portal in our pockets. So, if we are going to follow St. Paul down the path (and we should), as hungry men with robust sexual appetites (thank you biology and high T-counts!), we might do well to reconsider that Snickers bar we tote in our blue jeans left pocket. We just might think about it: *"IF I know I'm always hungry and IF I know that I love a Snickers bar and IF I know that those Snicker bars are an affront to my King and they are the death of me, then, by golly I'm going to do some serious soul-searching regarding this Snickers bar (a.k.a. cellular portal to the internet) I tote around."* It's about more than the boobs and butts on Instagram: it's about the first and last skirmish of every day. Losing those skirmishes impacts all the other aspects of our realm and increases vulnerability on other fronts. The miserably little defeats undercut my confidence and ability to step into confident command in the other spheres. When our hearts are weakened and compromised and we've not operated in authority over our appetites – we don't have confidence to wield authority elsewhere.

To sum up appetites: they are real. They are strong. Food hunger and sexual appetite are natural and good impulses, but they want to be the king in your life. They're so strong that the fight hardly seems fair. The only hope for a man who is serious about the King's reign in his heart is to submit to the King, create strong relationships with other men who fight like maniacs, and be willing to take radical measures to stop making opportunities for these appetites to consume you. Your life will look fundamentally different from your co-workers' if you take big steps toward obedience. Are you okay with that?

ADDICTIONS

The body has other addictions as well. We have friends who can't get off sugar, fast food, soda pops, high-end lattes, Little Debbie cake snacks. Our bodies want many things. We suspect we're going to have increasing numbers of men who begin to get very serious about how much they're drinking, about what that brown juice is soothing. Increasingly, we have conversations with men inside and outside our churches that are starting to own the fact that our body-cravings lead our soul around by the nose. We're encountering more and more men in the faith who are completely fine having a little dance with Mary Jane on the weekends because *"Hey, it's legal. I enjoy my Christian liberties and without the legal issues in my way, let's light 'em up! Don't be Mr. Grumpy."*

They are always shocked to hear a counterpoint from the Scriptures not related to the strict 'no dancing, no gambling, no tattoos' hyper-religious guidelines of the 1950s. An alert brain – the combat and governance mindset of a Kingdom-minded Viceroy – will instruct him to be battle-ready and poised for a victory at any minute. That's why we avoid drunkenness. That's why we don't want our faculties or senses dulled in ANY way. We've got too much riding on keeping our minds sharp that we swat marijuana and the third beer-of-the-night away rather quickly. The stakes are higher than they've ever been, and the King's reputation (not to mention, the welfare of our families) is at stake. We want Him to receive every honor, and it would pain us to dishonor Him by saying stupid things, making stupid choices, or failing to model righteousness, peace, and joy to my children or community. No thanks. Is there anything less 'royal' than enslavement to substances and digital sluts? We think this is slave thinking and we aren't to be mastered by any of it.

SOUL

Physical appetites (the body, our flesh) are only the start. New Testament writers thought in terms of body, soul (composed of the mind, the will, and emotions), and spirit. And guess what? All of these regions are coming under the King's banner as well. Our minds are going to be devoted and humble servants of the King. When our minds tell us things that oppose the King, we can tell them to stand down. Faith and obedience are great examples of 'mind-defying' postures. We don't mean to say we should always be violating our minds, but *my mind is not my ruler*. Christ the King is our ruler.

The King wants our minds to be transformed into a mind that thinks like the King. Here is an example from a Viceroy bro: *"Anytime the King asks me to take an action that violates my sensibilities regarding money, my obedience becomes an opportunity to worship Him."* A man who struggles with operational control of his finances – who can't make, manage, or bolt down to a budget – is daily presented a moment to defy his own thinking and bring it into the right alignment. Likewise, a man who is a penny-pinching miser will have every opportunity to yield to the King and give generously though it defies his compounding interest brain and his hands shake as he reaches into his wallet. *"Write a thousand dollar check to that man"* is not a welcomed command from the King, and our minds are equipped to mount a compelling counterpoint. What are you going to do, Viceroy? You're going to pull your pen and checkbook and you're going to whimper out a small prayer of thanksgiving that the King has been so generous to you! At this moment, you were able to bring all your faculties into Kingly alignment. Your mind said I SHOULDN'T, your will said NOPE, and your emotions squealed like a pig-tailed schoolgirl. But good job! You submitted and demonstrated allegiance to the King.

MONEY

And this naturally surfaces another bit of territory we haven't yet fully explored: your money. You probably remember the King said this in **Matthew 6:21**, *"For where your treasure is, there your heart will be also."* The big 'a-ha' about this verse is that your heart follows your money and not the other way around. It always seemed like the King's men would see a need or believe in a mission with their heart and then they would be 'moved' to invest their Kingdom dollars in the initiative: the missionary couple, the kids in Botswana, or the well in Kenya. But that isn't what the verse says. The opposite is true: your heart follows where you put your treasure, where you spend your money.

Watch this: if you invest in Ford Motor Company stock, you're suddenly going to care deeply about Ford Motors. You start putting $100 a month into a guy building the Kingdom in the Philippines and – wham-o! – you actually care to read his support letters and say prayers on his behalf. The trick for King's men is to ask good questions and find out who/what are good 'fields' to sow resources into and then double your investment. Seed that ground well! We should invest precious time and money in a guy we think is a good field, a guy who will be faithful to reproduce and steward resources well. We should not be as inclined to sow into a guy, even a minister, if we don't know much about him or his driving purpose. We can't afford to sling seeds (always limited) into places that won't prosper. We only want our hearts concerned with what is actually spreading, growing, advancing more of the Kingdom.

You can see we just described money as 'seed' – a Biblical concept, to be sure. But, in modern terms, money is fuel. It propels things forward. When you get more money, you can do more stuff. You can start new companies, partner up with other guys and start a non-profit that pushes more blessings into the earth. You can pour fuel into another person's tank so he can go after his Kingdom vision. You get to see things move because you put some coin behind the initiative. This idea of money as fuel is compelling and life-changing. Slowly, we King's men stop thinking, *"I want more money so I can buy an even bigger house and a ski-boat and get my wife a boob job"* and we start thinking, *"I want gobs more money and even a little bit more than that: I have real ambition to see Kingdom goals expanded. I'm greedy for fuel because I'm greedy to see the King's reputation grow; I'd love to steward even more resources before my flame blows out! I want to initiate three more partnership agreements with more Christian men and employ other young Christian men and see hundreds of households flourish."* Isn't that a different way of thinking than what the Prudential commercials are pushing on the TV? Retirement. Retirement. Retirement. It's so boring! Viceroys are very bored with this notion of 'retirement.' It just sounds too pathetic to even consider. Those waning years will be our most powerful, dynamic years. More on this in Chapter Nine.

We shouldn't wrap up a discussion about money without mentioning the verses that followed that 'heart and treasure' passage. **Matthew 6:24**, *"No one can serve two masters; for either he will hate the one and love the other, or else he will be loyal to the one and despise the other. You cannot serve God and mammon."* This verse does two interesting things. First, it highlights competing 'masters' for our allegiance, and there seems to be a real threat that our hearts will be led away in the wrong directions. Second, it calls money 'Mammon,' and this is likely from a Syrian word for the god of wealth and profit. It would make sense that the King would issue a warning for allowing your heart to grow in affection for wealth, even possibly personifying the demonic power behind wealth as 'Mammon,' a rival to the King's claim on your life. Conversely, the church has too long turned its nose up to wealth creation and accruing wealth. We propose that we regard money as fuel and seed. It simply powers forward and grows what is in our hearts. The reprobate playboy pagan who acquires more wealth just gets more hedonistic. When the King's men acquire wealth, they now have fuel for more projects that push blessings and benefits to more people. We would do well to periodically check in with the King and evaluate our relationship to money. Whatever this verse is saying, it at least implies that money (fuel) is corrosive, that it can contaminate if held too close to the heart for too long. It isn't value-neutral. Money isn't benign. It has coercive powers. We ought to put gloves and goggles on when we're dealing with it. Money is powerful stuff, and men love powerful stuff!

Finally, we ought to deal with that famous passage from **Matthew 19:**

"Then Jesus said to His disciples, 'Assuredly, I

say to you that it is hard for a rich man to
enter the kingdom of heaven. And again I say
to you, it is easier for a camel to go through
the eye of a needle than for a rich man to enter
the kingdom of God.' When His disciples
heard it, they were greatly astonished, saying,
'Who then can be saved?' But Jesus looked
at them and said to them, 'With men this is
impossible, but with God all things are
possible.'"

The point seems to be that it will take AN ACT OF GOD to get a rich man into the Kingdom. He is too inflated, too fat, too large in himself to enter into the narrowness of the Kingdom of Heaven; it will require too much stripping and death to too much of himself. It verges on the miraculous for a rich man to endure and submit when he has so much wealth. But notice one thing, it says nothing about a man who is in the kingdom and then... becomes wealthy. Our King isn't addressing that sequence. Those who already have the gospel and already know the King's heart, who work to align themselves with His intentions in the earth – who know His righteous order that establishes peace and joy – those men can become wealthy without trusting in their own abilities, ledger balances, or grandeur. We know full well who has given us the power to get wealth. We know how to be men under command. We will desire to push resources and invest-ment to others so the household of our Father King only continues its expansion. May it be so.

TIME & TECHNOLOGY

Kingdom men know that their time isn't their own any more than their breath or their relationships. Time is a gift. There was a time as much younger men when we had so much time on our hands it ran down our forearms and dripped off our elbows. We remember using phrases like 'just killing time' or 'burning a few hours.' It's hard to convince a 20-year-old that time is the most precious and critical resource he has. You can try it. It won't work. It sounds like a cliche to a young man who has never once felt the insufficiency of the hours. 20-year-olds enjoy a strange situation: maximum freedom with the least responsibility. Thankfully, they have the least amount of resources or things would quickly get out of hand!

Oddly, Americans complain about never having enough time to do all the things we need. A recent report by the RAND Corporation, a nonprofit research organization, says "Americans across all demographic groups enjoy an average of five hours of leisure time per day." That's way more than most of us would admit to enjoying. It sounds way off to me! But 'leisure' means time spent in ways unstructured or un-accounted for by work or home responsibilities. That is a lot of time we are filling with a thousand happy distractions.

We are – without a doubt – the most entertained people who have ever lived. Entire industries exist to make sure none of us are bored for even one hour in an airport (May it never be!). We wish we could tell you that it is an anomaly for us to have coffee with a young man only to learn he 'burns' 20 hours a week on video games. The necks and heads bowed in veneration of devices on subways and cafes mark our 'hours out' while binge-watching streaming episodes marks our 'hours in.' This is the modern moment.

If these descriptions hit home, we would ask you to pause and ask two important questions: *How much do I value my life? How much is an hour of my life worth?* Because the answers to these questions will likely explain why you are willing to see so many of them wash down the digital drain.

A life that is not sacred – ordained and designated by the King – is easily tossed away. The life that has purpose knows well the meaning of **Psalm 100**:

> *"Make a joyful shout to the Lord, all you lands!*
> *Serve the Lord with gladness; Come before*
> *His presence with singing. Know that the*
> *Lord, He is God; It is He who has made us,*
> *and not we ourselves; We are His people and*
> *the sheep of His pasture."*

A Viceroy has a deep understanding of this reality. Our worship comes in knowing that our lives are not our idea. We do not designate how many days we will each walk on this planet, and we shouldn't commit the slowest form of suicide by flittering away this life like a fast-food napkin whipped around northbound Interstate 45 during rush-hour traffic. Just as the moment of our birth is profound, and the moment of our death is deeply meaningful, so is our 2,496th Tuesday, and next Monday at 6:30 pm. That day and that hour will also be significant. We are men on assignment in a hostile land: we are the King's men doing serious work in the earth that will move like a shockwave into the future. So, no, we did not Netflix binge-watch season six of that thriller. We were doing stuff.

In fact, we would all do well to remember the final exam alluded to in **I Corinthians 3:12-15**. See, it's kinda like we all give a great big presentation at the end of this joyride we call a lifespan. We set it all out on a big folding table and present all the stuff we did to the King as He sits in His judgment seat, and then it all gets torched – incinerated. A massive bonfire happens with the product of our lives, and season six of the murder-mystery thriller probably goes up in smoke while the lives you blessed endure. It's a stunning moment, I'm sure! No doubt – many folks will walk away from the inferno thinking "I did not see that coming" or "That didn't go well." Others will certainly have stacks of gold remaining. Surely, you can see that time management and hours invested actually mean something. Viceroys know how to manage the resources entrusted to them. Once you hear the ticking clock deep in your psyche, it is always there – faint, but always there. Technology serves us; we don't serve it. If it needs to stay locked in a closet on weekends – just so it learns its place – so be it. We won't allow something that needs to be so frequently re-charged rob us of days gifted by the Crown of Eternity.

CHAPTER 6
HOUSEHOLD

THE ATTACK ON THE HOUSEHOLD

A VICEROY GUY REMEMBERS: *"To my knowledge, there's no SUPER-PAC, no international plot, or super-secret cabal in a darkened room plotting the steady decline of the traditional American family. I grew up in the eighties where 'the war on the American family' was a commonly-stated belief and constant reference point. The assumption was that Hollywood, Washington, and all the Federal Courts were a sort of 'axis of evil' funded by the Kremlin perhaps or the Rothschilds or ... the dark lord – Lucifer himself, bent on the destruction of my family and yours. Madonna and MTV were likely involved as well, though to what degree – we might only guess.*

"All of this may be true – Soros, the Davos devils, Bill Gates – who knows what they're doing right now; frankly it's exhausting to speculate about it. The truth is, I doubt any clandestine organization or transnational plot is necessary at all. We seem to be speedily face-planting just fine on our own. We have a real spiritual Enemy - no doubt, but he's crafty enough to help us self-destruct. That's my take, anyway."

Our King's enemy is also our enemy. We know that governments and mega-corporations and even local school boards are fundamentally opposed to the King's governance on the earth. There are territorial powers that resist good men and virtuous homesteads; in short, the struggle is real. We know that the household is 'tactical' as C.R. Wiley has said – the household is a weapon deployed to take territory in the King's name. It will be resisted, but you're just the man the King has in mind to lead an assault team. You run a household. If you've never read C.R. Wiley's two books, *The Household and the War for the Cosmos* and *Man of the House* – do yourself a favor and drop them into your shopping cart right away. These are two of the best books you'll ever read regarding what happens under your roofline – a roofline that matters.

YOUR ROOF MATTERS – PAY ATTENTION

The King's men know what we've always known – unless the LORD builds the house, we labor in vain. **Psalms 127 & 128** are key household Psalms that contain a treasure trove of household images perfectly crafted for guiding our thinking; we will reference them throughout this chapter. Regarding 'unless the LORD builds the house,' the verse shows you can knock yourself out, running this way and that – never missing a baseball game and always saying our evening prayers and being good disciplinarians and you ARE NOT guaranteed great kiddos or a flourishing household as the outcome. There is a good bit of dependence on the King to see our households through to faithful completion. We've known incredibly wise men, good stewards through and through, who had children who departed from the right paths – some of whom never returned. What are we to do with that? *Proceeding in faith* is always the right answer when the counter-evidence seems overwhelming. Faith, it seems, is the currency of the Kingdom. We step out and believe and rack up deficits wherein we've banked everything on the King being true to His word and faithful in His deliverance. All the footings are bolted to that Rock and the storms won't prevail. There isn't any back-up plan for a Viceroy.

A Viceroy knows that if it happens under his roofline – it belongs to him alone. Every event is his victory, his defeat, his problem, his pain. That teenager who got busted with a joint off-campus. That belongs to a father. The wife who is struggling with depression, well, that isn't just 'her problem.' Whatever our children watch on an iPad – that's on us. Radical responsibility means that it will cost us dearly to stay extremely 'tuned in' and vigilant. The 4.0-grade point your 12-year-old daughter earns – that's partly yours! You didn't study the Eastern European geography terms, but the daughter of your household earned that under your roof and the King is faithfully building your household day by day.

A note here about trusting institutions to do your job: *don't do that*. At this late date, well into the 21st century, we should all be disabused of the notion that the old structures are up to the task of raising our children. Here's what we mean. We can't tell you how many men have said something like this to us in a training: *"I don't know what happened, this came out of the blue – we had him in a Christian school, she was in a good group of friends, we had a filtering service on our home wireless network, it happened on a church youth group retreat of all places, he was in Boy Scouts, we were paying for a respected counselor..."* Farming out the deeper parts of raising our sons and daughters simply doesn't work anymore, and it never has.

Viceroys are looking for ways to invest in the King's model of household management – a clue is found in the aforementioned **Psalm 128:**

> *Blessed is everyone who fears the Lord,*
> *Who walks in His ways.*
> *When you eat the labor of your hands,*
> *You shall be happy, and it shall be well with you.*
> *Your wife shall be like a fruitful vine*
> *In the very heart of your house,*
> *Your children like olive plants*
> *All around your table.*
> *Behold, thus shall the man be blessed*
> *Who fears the Lord.*

PRIORITY ONE

First, we get a blessing by walking according to the ways of the King – by fearing His name only. We like the sound of that. That is goal number one around here. Priority one! Because priority one comes with a wonderful outcome – we get to enjoy happiness and blessings (that is a word that means – *it will be well with you* – in all the ways we can conceive of prosperity). It just almost sounds like those three elements of the Kingdom – right? Righteousness, peace, and joy? Yes sir, priority number one – honor the King.

WIFE WINE

Second, a wife gets a sheltered blessing and a place of honor in the interior of our households. She is cherished, nurtured, and cared for like we would care for a fruitful vine that makes the sweetest wine. Children should be constantly amazed at how well we speak of our wife and honor her with words and deeds. Our mouths should be set to 'rapid-fire praise' of a beautiful, strong, intelligent, funny, and graceful wife. This kind of soil and this kind of shelter gives her the best chance to produce fruit. She is a blessing to our house financially and builds a sweet, nourishing culture within these walls. If we ran our operations without her – it would likely look more like a Ford assembly line than a place where children laugh and learn and play and grow into well-rounded adults. Men are rubbish at the kind of work that comes so naturally to a beautiful, engaged wife.

You might notice here that the struggle with nurturing a wife in this manner really rests in the basins of our own hearts as men. It's true. This compromised heart, tutored by this world, will tend to appraise the worth of a wife wrongly. We might compare her to some manufactured 'ideal' we have of a wife. We might think she is a sorry housekeeper, not as good a cook as our own mother, or not as beautiful or trim as the bright shiny young lady on the magazine cover in the check-out line. Men often appraise our wives wrongly, and we create an inner dialogue that occasionally bleeds out to destroy her self-estimation and our intimacy. Regardless of how well you think you conceal this internal script, I assure you it will leak out soon enough and often at just the WRONG moment. When you speak words of life to her, over her, and about her, you will watch her bloom and strengthen and endure any number of difficult circumstances. **Ephesians 5:28** says *"he who loves his wife loves himself."*

By the way – this is the way of the King. Check out **Ephesians 5:27** –

> *"that He [the King] might present her [us, His bride] to Himself a glorious church, not having spot or wrinkle or any such thing, but that she should be holy and without blemish."*

We get to enter into a Kingly heart position every day we enter our house from a hard day's work and embrace our wife and tell her how much we love her and thank her for her hard work with the kids that day. But the work, the inside work in our heart, starts by not accusing her or measuring her against a different standard. We get to *'present her as perfect'* to our own mind. We can choose to present her as perfect in our own estimating – in our ways of thinking. She isn't, of course – she isn't *perfect*. But – and this is important – we can *present* her to our mind as though she is. Rather than accusing or diminishing her value, we can esteem her and care for her.

A Viceroy chimes in: *"If I do anything, say anything, that puts questions into her mind about how she looks (weight, hair, clothing, etc.) – I only fertilize the weeds that seek to choke out her wellbeing. I would be a fool. I would actively work against my own interest by injuring the fruitful vine in my home. Yet I meet so many men who do precisely this – by giving slashing remarks in their exasperation. Do this, speak to your wife in this way, to your own destruction."*

The ramifications are significant. She struggles with not measuring up, whether she says it or not. She sees the same magazines you do. She knows that the third kid wrecked her body. She worries about calories more than you do (probably). She worries she isn't sexy enough to keep your interest – she reads the horror stories online. Your steady, rock-stable confidence in her, the affirmation of her, and esteem directed at her will stabilize and fortify her soil. She will bloom and fruit and your household will be the sweetest 2K square feet on the block. Her wine will soothe and numb a thousand difficult hours and tumultuous days. Be a good vine-keeper and your days are much better off. A mature, established vine – a heritage vine – is precious and renowned the world over. The vineyards of Bordeaux and Burgundy in France are a horticultural wonder. We've met many seasoned women of the King's order who fit the same description – we know the wives of men in central Texas do. If your wife seems like she is miles away from this description, then proceed in faith. Trust and pray that God will do transformative work in her heart and you keep sacrificially investing in her, encouraging her and walking with her in patience. Your resolve and love (the bit you can control) will pay dividends in the years ahead.

If your wife is stubborn and won't submit to your leadership (I've heard it happens), then this is where you persevere, submit to your spiritual leadership, and continue to love and lead in humility. You may be in for a decade of work (or more) as you earn her trust, practice gentleness, and refuse to throw in the towel or shirk your governing responsibilities. You might go through the ringer as you learn to love and govern and shepherd your wife. A Viceroy bro jumps in: *"Here's a key paragraph that helped break open some communication with my wife, as a very young married couple — 'Babe, I have a responsibility to shepherd and care for you. That word shepherd is connected to sheep, of course. I have to tell you that every time I approach you to give you good food, or remove a burr, or help you back on your feet – it feels like you bite my fingers. Honestly, it makes me not want to shepherd, care, lead, or even converse with you. It makes my figurative 'fingers' kinda hurt. I also know that you probably, deep down, want me to continue to shepherd you in this life we're walking together. Can you think about this and let's talk about it next weekend?'"*

OLIVE PLANT CHILDREN

> *"Your children like olive plants – all around your table."* **Psalm 128:3**

The first thing to note is that olive trees aren't naturally positioned around tables. Olive trees are small trees that flourish in the Mediterranean region, but the Psalmist's depiction of olive plants stationed under a roof and around the table is significant because it says something about the house manager. These are likely young saplings – off-shoots without deeply established roots. A table is a place of feeding, nourishment, delight, and warmth inside away from the elements. This man has intentionally and carefully created a sort of 'hot-house' by which the young plants can grow to some level of maturity. They won't always be around the table, they will be transplanted and will soon have to reckon with the heat of the day and the frost of the winter, but in the days of youth – they are kept close and indoors and tenderly nourished. This is a fantastic picture of what we are doing when we raise children.

To be clear – we don't mean that we are hyper-protective, obsessive, worry-ridden bores about every detail of their lives. This is a common stance, especially in our modern moment with the influx of information. It can drive young parents batty. Just toss out *'vaccinations/anti-vax'* at the next company social and watch people flop on the floor in hysterics on both sides of the issue.

It doesn't mean we keep children from any and all stress. Part of root development is exposure to stress. We stunt kids if we attempt to fully 'shelter' them. That said, the common swipe at home-school kids is that they are 'SHELTERED' and thus unable to deal with the real world. We've met these kids. You've likely met these kids. It isn't pretty – in fact, it is painfully awkward to observe them in their natural state. Our own home-school kids make jokes about 'home-school' kids!

But we are always very suspicious of an attitude that says – *"well, we just want our kids to be lights in the public schools"* or *"we don't want weirdo kids who can't relate to other kids their age – we thought homeschooling would do that to them."* First of all, are you saying that your kids have a working faith, personal identity structure, and Biblical foundation stones sufficient to handle whatever 7th grade throws at them? That is impressive. Your kids are little scripture spouting missionaries ready to suffer any hardship like Paul and Silas in the Philippian jail? Dang. Hats off to you, amigo! Those are some impressive root systems that won't wilt in the face of a 10th-grade study hall when the upperclassmen pass around the phone with the porn video. Very good rooting, indeed.

A Viceroy guy chimes in: *"As a former public school teacher, I can tell you this: weird parents have weird kids. Mark it well. I don't care what context you examine – public, private, parochial, college-prep, or home-school – weirdos create weirdo homes and children warp under their leadership. Educators see it every day, and that pattern is rarely (but yes, occasionally) reversed."*

Our children stand a much higher chance of embracing and replicating your household culture the more time they spend working through daily situations and rehearsing family statements (family mission and key phrases) and logging hours around the family table. This works for the good and the bad. Chuck them into a different culture in their formative years and other kinds of plants begin to graft into them. You will be forced to do a bit of extra work pruning out, cutting off, and re-routing branches. It is hard work and it requires serious engagement and discipline on the parent's part – but it is possible. Building a strong family culture is the best nutrition and fortification against disease and pestilence and frostbite on the leaves. Your table is your best location, your highest and best use of square feet in your home; we've somehow forgotten or lost this truth somewhere along the way. Recover it. Get a big table. Use it often. Talk and talk and talk and invite others into your table and let children learn how to engage in conversation and discuss film, literature, and politics in a place their roots can stretch out. The withering and blistering assault will wait for them – they'll face their trials soon enough. But today – in these precious few years of formation – these olive plants will receive the attention that should secure our one-day orchard.

BLESSINGS OF FEARING THE KING

We grow these vines and these little plants in our homes out of obedience and because we believe there will be a fruitful outcome. It is costly – if you choose to homeschool (and you probably should – you want YOUR culture woven into their DNA), for example, you face tremendous out of pocket expenses (co-op fees, books, museums, supplies) and loss-of-earning costs for the household as a whole. Is it worth it? You have to decide for yourself. Those who don't homeschool or private school (there should be some big, insurmountable variable that demands this kind of sacrifice of your household) – you face a herculean task to make sure you are re-seeding and watering to match the stresses your kids face outside your walls. It is rigorous and demanding work no matter which path you choose, but Viceroys say the King's pleasure is worth it and the harvest is worth it.

THE OUTCOME OF PROTECTED/TRAINED CHILDREN

> *Behold, children are a heritage from the Lord,*
> *The fruit of the womb is a reward.*
> *Like arrows in the hand of a warrior,*
> *So are the children of one's youth.*
> *Happy is the man who has his quiver full of them;*
> *They shall not be ashamed,*
> *But shall speak with their enemies in the gate.*

Psalm 127:3-5

This Psalm of instruction was either penned by King David for his son Solomon or was written by Solomon himself. In either case – this is a royal household text and one we should pay attention to. It is referenced so often in faith communities that it may sound trite and threadbare. Let's agree together that this is a declaration about the value of children – in an age that devalues children. I'll never forget the derision and looks of disgust when we brought our four children into a trendy restaurant in San Francisco. Increasingly, our culture values 'fur babies' over children, for all the obvious reasons. Our birth rate plunges as a result. But the King declares children are good and He gathers children to Himself. In fact, we are *rewarded* when we give birth to children. Why are they a reward? Weird thought: children are ammunition.

DISCLAIMER:

I should probably jump in and address the 'quiver-full' movement that is swirling around (and parodied widely by our cultural adversaries). When you read up on this movement, even a cursory reading on Wikipedia, you see that most of the underlying assumptions are perfectly in step with our King's mandate: fill the earth, reproduce, nurture, expand, receive blessing through offspring, many children are a good thing. There are excesses in that movement. A woman's value is NOT limited to her childbearing abilities. Your wife likely has a brilliant mind as well and she should be applauded for using it! Having 17 children will create a unique family environment and the neighbors will talk – but it isn't clear from the Scriptures that every family must fill an entire transit van. Families that adopt are not 'less blessed' because they didn't 'fruit' from their own womb, etc. Some of the fringe elements of the 'quiver-full movement' are really unusual expressions of the King's body – and we will leave it at that. Birth control and family planning are incendiary topics, deeply personal, and guided by various teachings of the church – consult your spiritual leadership about that topic and get their input. We're not offering that here. It is sufficient here to emphasize that children are good! You should want as many as you and your wife can possibly manage. They offer both obvious and hidden blessings. We often say that a wife is the most effective tool the King uses to 'rough hew' a man's edges and angles. Each child feels like a different grit rating of sandpaper. Child by child, year by year – we've been changed and these hearts are a little smoother and refined as a result.

Back to the 'children of one's youth' being ammunition – they are sent out into the world to do damage. An arrow is not a multi-purpose instrument. You don't *also* use arrows to hang the laundry or herd sheep or fix an alternator. An arrow is a weaponized amalgam of wood, stone, and feathers for fletching. An arrow is sent to maim and prepare for the kill. If it is a well-constructed and well-formed arrow, it will be effective many times over. Whereas a rifle round can be deployed once, an archer can pull an arrow and re-launch at whatever next target might emerge – launched, that is, with deadly precision.

Viceroys expect that their children will be a deployable

family asset – an arrow aimed at a problem, an adversary, a venture that needs to be subdued. The same way that the King inherently trusts the Viceroy to carry out His mission on earth, a father should be able to trust a son or daughter to send them on behalf of the family to effect change. We see less of this today, but it used to be common to walk into an establishment, a lending institution for example, and have an older man shake your hand and say, *"You're Tom's boy, aren't you. What can I do for you?"* The reputation of the elder established enough good footing that business is transacted easier.

A Viceroy guy speaks up: *"I'll never forget walking into a tractor parts-supplier to pick up a bushing for my grandfather's cotton picker. The man at the counter handed me the part and told me to 'have a good day.' I asked about making payment and he said, 'You're Ransom's boy, right? Well, I just figured I'd add it to his account this afternoon.' That seems like a scene from a different century; today transactions happen through automated phone trees and software. But I will tell you that if a young man approached me with a resume and I knew he had been trained by a Viceroy – I do believe I'd accept him on those grounds alone. If only there was such a network of men in place... hmm. We really should get on that; it might just be a more compelling network than LinkedIn."*

Lastly, it may be worth considering one other implication of sending an arrow to speak with an enemy. The city gates were the place of political, civil, economic, and religious debate in historic communities. In ancient Israel, a man had to be thirty years old to sit at the gates, and even then, he was likely (using his wisdom) to remain silent as the elders conversed. He had a seat, but age and experience were esteemed much higher in that culture at that time than they are today. Arrows are precision-strike instruments. This is about releasing astute tacticians – wise negotiators who can read people, know their numbers, and identify good opportunities. That is the kind of mind that should be sent into a 'heated' moment with an enemy at the gate. This kind of 'arrow' uses knowledge, understanding, and wisdom to drive to the heart of the adversary. May we all raise as many of these men and women as possible.

LAST THOUGHT – WHAT DO I BUILD SPECIFICALLY INTO SONS VS. DAUGHTERS?

King David says something else that should direct our understanding of how we are to be raising our sons and daughters. This is a description of how the Great High King brings blessings to His people's households – and saves kings. Listen up – that's you, Viceroy!

Psalm 144 states:

> *I will sing a new song to You, O God;*
> *On a harp of ten strings, I will sing praises*
> *   to You,*
> ***The One who gives salvation to kings,***
> *Who delivers David His servant*
> *From the deadly sword.*
> *Rescue me and deliver me from the hand of*
> *   foreigners,*
> *Whose mouth speaks lying words,*
> *And whose right hand is a right hand of*
> *   falsehood—*

*That **our sons may be as plants grown up in
        their youth**;*
*That **our daughters may be as pillars,
Sculptured in palace style**;*
That our barns may be full,
Supplying all kinds of produce;
That our sheep may bring forth thousands
And ten thousands in our fields;
That our oxen may be well laden;
That there be no breaking in or going out;
That there be no outcry in our streets.

The marker of sons raised in royal households is early maturity – not prolonged adolescence. Plants that are *grown up in their youth* means that they assume responsibility early and manage themselves; they distinguish themselves as mature young men earlier than their peers. That is a marker of a king-caliber young man. The defining characteristic of kingly daughters is that they remind observers of finely *sculptured palace pillars.* Consider this: of course young women from Viceroy homes are beautiful. That's a given – they ought to be confident of their value in the deepest parts of their soul. They are also strong – holding up under significant weight and responsibility of the palace and household. This also speaks to stability. They are steady and unwavering, as any good pillar should be.

Ponder this question: is this the depiction of most 17-year-old sons or daughters in your city? We doubt that it is. Early maturity that shoulders the weight of responsibility for self and others? Are women praised equally for their beauty, strength, and unshakable emotional poise? Or are they pink haired screamers, pierced and mouthy? That shouldn't be the case in our households. We know 30-year-old women who are an emotional riot mob, 30-year-old men who shouldn't be trusted with anything more than crossing the street, and 60-year-old pop stars who still parade their saggy skin on a stage as though their only value exists in their cankerous sex appeal (we didn't use Madonna's name, but you know who we're talking about). Our homes should be building these kinds of kingly young people and by the King's grace and power, Viceroys endeavor to do just that.

CHAPTER 7

COMPETITORS TO YOUR HOUSEHOLD

* **Disclaimer:** We know there are extenuating circumstances and unique variables in everyone's life. We recognize that we are painting with broad brush-strokes in this chapter, and that every couple must sort through their particular circumstances. Infertility is a real thing. Miscarriages happen. Economic realities can be downright beastly! Rather than count us reactionary or insensitive, just know that we're addressing macro-trends across our culture and speaking to a heart posture that affirms our role as Kingly stewards – as Viceroys.

THE VERY FIRST thing to note is that our current cultural understanding of the household is rather recent, extremely skewed, and a shabby stand-in for what households are and can be. When I speak to young men, typically college students and the under-thirty professional crowd, there seems to be little interest in quickly getting married and jumping into the raising of children. In fact, children are often the furthest thing from their minds – following well behind quick career establishing, advancing, possibly getting hitched, or a 'place of our own.' This creates an extremely delayed timeline for getting a household filled with snotty-nosed little creatures who whine and throw their toys. Painting the picture of a household full of diapers and spit-up rags, a tired Medusa-haired wife in a bathrobe, and a mortgage payment makes many a young man head for the hills.

We much prefer an idealized sequence that would run something like this: *get the career started, maybe make one or two advancements, get the savings accounts well established, find a girl (a real knock-out, of course) with her own earning potential, get a dog – probably a responsibly harvested rescue pup, get the starter home fixed up – spend the disposable income on great weekend trips to Boston and Seattle, get a legit 4-wheel drive camping rig, set up a home-brew operation for me and my buddies, finally – somewhere in mid to late 30's have 'a' kid, or possibly 'two' kids and then shut down the power-plant with a vasectomy just before March Madness week. Get the little ones into a decent daycare program or pre-school and enjoy the benefits of having finally landed that house in the blue-ribbon school district. Sure, there's going to be some dicey moments in those 20 years of raising kids, sure. But the wife wants 'em, and I'm going to need to be able to fill a Thanksgiving table when I'm wearing my sweaters in old age, I guess. It's what we do, right? Eventually? We all bite the bullet and have kids. How bad can it be, right?*

We have a Viceroy buddy – a 28-year-old friend Michael, who casually dropped the idea that he had four kids by the same wife. (He now has six and is 32. Who knows how many will eventually show up!) We sat around a campfire full of dudes and watched eyes grow as big as dinner plates while two of them started choking on the beers they accidentally inhaled.

Nobody does this! Why? Why would anyone agree to start having a bus-full of kids in their early 20's? It's irresponsible. It's a recipe for disaster. It's resigning yourself to the most depressing lifestyle imaginable. You would have to be independently wealthy – a trust fund kid, maybe, to make such a decision. Even then – those little buggers will scream and wreck your wife's body and end your tranquility. No thank you. Go sell 'crazy' somewhere else, amigo!

We swear we're not overstating the point. These are very common responses to radical pro-family decisions. Rational, self-interested young men would never choose to lock themselves into that kind of weight, responsibility, options-limiting home structure. Accidents happen, of course, but to choose it?!

Never!

So what made our friend Michael do such a thing? He is bright, handsome according to all the females polled: tall, dark-haired, bearded, fit – he works in mid-management for a major company. Clever and funny. Kind. He is 'officer caliber' in every respect – no matter the situation, he is calm and clear thinking. And he must be BANANAS!

No. Michael has a great father. That father of his gave him a secret formula that was passed down to him. It feels ancient, in many respects, but it is time-tested. His formula is seasoned with perspective.

The formula starts like this.

First, let's take a critical look at the current script – the smart-American script we outlined above – the dog and 4x4 and good schools, etc. That script places the single man's desires at the top of the decision tree. It asks almost nothing of him – the career is his to chisel as he pleases. The girl is his to take or wed or use until the point that she threatens to leave him. Should she be the sort of woman who WANTS a child (all the better for him if she doesn't), then he only concedes after delaying to the last possible moment. If children are considered a 'gift' to him – they are only considered such because they are 'little buddies' and it means even more baseball on Saturdays. Teenage years are something to endure until they get into a good school and make the Christmas cards more impressive. And! The other kinda great thing about those kids is that they might help me in my late years when I'm feeble. End of story. This script prioritizes the delay of responsibility above all and is the very definition of 'short-vision.'

Second, let's look at the older man's advice to his son. Remember, the son has no idea what is best for him, what really matters in this life, how quickly time flies, the costs and benefits of hard decisions. He just doesn't, because none of us do when we start out. The true assessments come only with hindsight – in retrospect we see. The gift of perspective is what older men can give us if we shut up and pay attention and pose thoughtful questions while heeding what they say.

The older man's advice is that youth, vitality, and character-formation are part and parcel with getting a young wife and strapping (duct-taping?) kids all over your body – front slings, backpacks, leashes, strollers, wagons. You will never have the energy you do in your twenties and early thirties. Your rest will never be better than slogging through the fatigue of toddler years. 50-year-old men who start second families for whatever reason – they know deep fatigue! Despite the oft-repeated maxim that the single years are the time to play the field and have lots of romantic experiences so you can find out what you like or need in a mate, and despite the adage that the first 3 to 4 years of marriage are when we learn so much about one another before the kids get here and it's time to start a family, guys who know the value of family – gray-haired Viceroys – will tell you most of that stuff is rubbish. Time is precious, fleeting, and often misappropriated.

Do not fear getting tied down to a wife. You get tied into a marriage and that is a very good thing – it begins to sort you out! You will never have more opportunities to discover your shortcomings, your pride, and your selfishness than when you get married. The children raise the stakes of the game, and the refining rounds move more quickly. They increase your opportunity to die to yourself – think of them as maturity accelerators.

Shocking insight: our friend Michael says he wishes they would have started sooner! They joke about ten kids – but they say they're taking it slow. Most of the big pushback around this sort of thinking rests with the considerations surrounding 'double-incomes' and career development. In Texas, we say it like this: *raising all these kids means you gotta cut a lot of hay*. They're expensive. No doubt about it.

The imagined damage to your career is another consideration you may just have to sort out with the King. We don't know what to tell you. A Viceroy guy testifies: *"This weekend I received word that a boyhood friend of mine left his established career, moved cities, and started over at the bottom of a new company because he chose to prioritize his relationship with his wife – who is struggling with mental health issues and likely was involved in infidelity. This guy is handling his situation like a champ – at tremendous personal cost and discomfort, he is placing his family's well-being over his own by taking a lowly position and fighting through the hardship. I'm proud of him!"*

Placing your career on the table before the King says He gets to make the decisions, but if you choose your employment and career path over all other factors (as we tend to do – as directed by the typical script) others will suffer and you'll end up with much less than you bargained for.

Where did Michael's father get this counter-cultural script? It is the collective wisdom of generations. At the end of a man's life, as he faces a terminal illness or the long goodbye, he never mentions his business achievements. You should encourage any immature young man who thumps his chest about being a DINK family (double income, no kids) to go spend an afternoon in a chemotherapy waiting room full of aging, sick people alone without active assistance from loved ones. It's crazy depressing. At the end of his life, he will need all those kids he didn't have! Old men reflect back on relationships that mattered. They count their grown children as the best of their life's work. Obituaries won't mention the 3rd quarter of 2019 – when Tom blew all the sales projections out of the water and the Miami office called to congratulate him. Why? Because it doesn't matter nearly as much as all the people you built into along the way – people in your high-power company included. When a good man dies at the end of his story, the family feels the mammoth void and the community where he lived is somehow poorer in his absence. His church misses the benefit of his perspective, and young men don't yet have the diamonds that formed in the old man over so much time and pressure. That matters. This insight is NOT immediately perceived at the age of 25; it can't be seen from such a distance.

Your children won't see what you're fighting to protect. It's beyond them. When they want to head out with friends on a Friday night and skip the evening Sabbath meal – a weekly tradition that celebrates their mother and rest and our role as King's sons – they won't see it as 'a big deal because we do it every week!' They can't see their lives at age 36 when they build traditions into their own homes because they remember it as the finest part of any week. They won't see that the technology restrictions are meant to do more than curtail the digital 'teen culture' pulsing into their gigabyte brains, they can't know that we are protecting brother and sister time that will make the critical welding joints such that they endure the stresses of time and distance as adult friends. How could they know?!

Another thing worth considering, just considering! We're not telling you what to do, but we have seen families over-commit themselves to a particular endeavor – a school, a sport, even a church – in a way that neglects household formation, rhythms, and good order. It's rare to find families with that much commitment, to be honest, but it happens occasionally. Worse than that – they might level the accusation that 'you, sir have made an idol of your home!' We can see why they might think that. In a world that deprioritizes and devalues strong homes, we might appear to be overly-fixated on hearth and home. It doesn't take long, however, over a coffee, to draw the lines that point back to our King and His vision for our children's long-term success and the impactful blast radius these young men and women will surely have in the earth and under the King's banner! Their training and equipment are not a fool's errand and should be a top priority. We're not 'fetishizing' our families – we're not high on some sort of Nestle's Toll-house cookie advertisement with Norman Rockwell characters depicting the 'idealized' Thanksgiving dinner table. As soon as you idealize anything, you'll be disappointed and surprised at what actually unfolds. Our lives and families never quite look like our fantasies; that isn't the point. As Viceroys, we look to our King and build into people as much of the Kingdom foundations as we possibly can. We trust the King with the outcome. We can't do anything more and He expects nothing less.

You might be assessing this chapter and thinking, *"Okay, fine – lot's of kids as early as possible. Weird flex. It seems like an odd thing to take a stand on, but whatever, man. You do you."* We don't have to view it the same way, but consider this: we want to govern as much as we can reasonably manage. And then we want a little bit more! We're greedy like that. If the King is handing out assignments, talents, acreage, whatever – we want to be first across that line. We're the guys grabbing extra baskets, extra vessels to hold anything the King is willing to pour out. It is implied in the parable that two talents are more desirable than one talent, and so on.

The foundational lie we've most recently come to believe in the West is that children are *not* inherently good. Children are a burden, an expense, a hiccup rather than a blessing. More children cannot possibly equal more bless-ings – they create more headaches and mess and noise. There are a hundred reasons why an 'enlightened mind' would be able to construct the counter-narrative to the King's position. But we are wrong, even foolish – we don't see rightly. If the King makes a declaration and you choose against that decree because you see the matter differently, you haven't just 'taken a different approach' or 'arrived at a different conclusion.' Your rebellion is no small matter – defiance of a king is called 'sedition.' Rather, we would be wise to repent of such lies, mindsets, and hardness of heart, and ask the King for mercy. That would be very smart and you would benefit in ways you can only guess at from this distance.

Lastly, as a matter of perspective, imagine a man at age 49 with say 5 children who are grown, released as arrows, and out of the house?! Though it may not seem so to a young man, a 49-year-old man has quite a few miles left on his drivetrain. Seasoned, trustworthy, softened by the sustained kindness of the King, in a marriage that is solid and sweet – what can that man do? What are his honed capabilities? Why that man is a dynamo! He builds layer by layer, brick by brick, into his grandchildren, younger men in the Kingdom, young fathers, and he can travel wherever directed by the King. He is capable of laying a considerable amount of foundation and he has perspective enough to know his body will fail him before his spirit will. He will make haste. The rocking chair on the porch can wait! This man, like our friend Michael, knew that jumping into the father game early was a good call. It yielded manifold blessings and outrageous crops in many fields. That Viceroy knew *he was the fight* – it was about his heart. He had to keep it refreshed by the King, stoked with love for his wife, and sacrificial for others. He wins because the King wins.

Oh. And just so you know – we've seen churches that demand things of families in such a way that they work at counter-purposes to a man's vision for his family. Seriously. Churches can demand over-commitments and thereby over-step the God-given boundaries. Your church should be a place that your family plugs in to learn to serve, to worship among the saints, and to hear the Scriptures taught authoritatively. You should trust the leadership of those in charge, AND it should augment, not detract, from your family mission and the culture you're building at your home address.

We won't go into too much detail here, but if select sport teams are running your wife, household, and children ragged – ditch 'em! The sports obsession in the US can absolutely work at cross-purposes with good, healthy family rhythms. We know they learn discipline and teamwork and how to govern emotions; we get it, but we've also seen families that look shredded by the toll the out-of-town games and 'multiple teams for every kid' circus can expect from an otherwise balanced and happy home. Keep an eye on it. One sport per kid isn't a bad rule of thumb – remember, *they aren't going pro.* A pro career is almost a statistical impossibility – don't let that dream run your home.

CHAPTER 8
OPERATIONS

WOW – you made it to chapter eight! OR – you skipped here once you read the Table of Contents. It's cool. It doesn't bother us. We're fine. Really.

There has likely been a lingering question forming somewhere in the back of your mind; it might be vague, even shrouded but you get the impression that something is *off* about the picture we've been painting together – the picture of the Viceroy mandate seems off. OR you may be very well tuned in to exactly what the problem is: you went to it straight away like a diamond-tipped drill bit through green jello.

MONEY!

The problem is finances and career. After all, this is why the draw of the large salary and the corner office and pension plan makes sense. It is alluring. Simply exchanging insane numbers of hours of your life (and likely your wife's hours as well) for financial security is the obvious call here. It isn't rocket science. Get a better job and make your moves – network and advance. You could draw this on a cocktail napkin for a 10th grader to understand!

So assuming you are not financially independent (trust funds, etc.) and assuming you aren't interested in living in a clothing-optional hippy commune where you forage for your food and bury your own crap in the woods as your many children roam free and stick dandelions in their wild hair – how are you going to pull this off? Money is no small consideration. It's a tough nut to crack.

AS AN EMPLOYEE

How a Viceroy runs his operation is a critical consideration. First, let's discuss how a Viceroy might function as a faithful employee. Especially when in the early phases of life – as a young man acquiring skill sets and business acumen – you will be answering to 'direct reports' and 'lead_____' and 'operating officers.' If you're in education, you will snap to attention before department heads or committees and boards. Wherever you are, you likely start in a subordinate role and then gain the trust and respect of your managers who want to give you more responsibility, position, and pay. That's just kinda how it works. I'm sure you've noticed.

A Viceroy operates off one key belief: *I work for the King.* I honor the authorities in my work, community, and nation of course, but I'm the King's man at the end of the day. His pleasure is my one concern. Obedience to Him trumps all other concerns or variables.

A Viceroy dude speaks up: *"When I ran a department many years ago, there were several 'Viceroy' kind of men in that* department – men who really knew the King and were excellent at their job. We met every week to talk shop and to pray. Over time, one of the men was promoted to Senior Director over the rest of us and I was his number two in charge of the rest. This shake-up could have created any number of awkward interactions. If we hadn't had the key understanding that the real boss of all of our hearts and our department was the King, it would have been difficult.

"But see, many years before we had discussed this truth: if we work every day and keep the King as the primary focus, an employer won't have a thing to document in the 'needs improvement' category of the yearly report. We will hit our KPI's. He or she will simply see that we give outrageous effort – that we go above and beyond to handle our responsibilities and even look to assist in areas not assigned. That is the rule of our life under the Crown.

"When my colleague was promoted and became my boss, I went to his office and said, 'Tom – I'm glad you got the job. They couldn't have picked a better man if they'd taken twice as long to look. I'm glad to be on your team and even though we have a friendship – I won't ever allow our friendship to distort your role as my boss. If you have a problem with me, my decisions, or actions at any point, I'm sure you will let me know and I will happily make whatever changes you require. No hard feelings. You'll always get a yes sir outta me.' I know Tom appreciated that because I appreciated it when other employees in our friend group approached me with the same sentiments as I was promoted above them. Kingly order creates good order when men (and women, of course) snap into correct alignment and look to honor others and the King."

We tell young men, early in their careers, to never do the bare minimum amount of work required in the job description. The organization that hired you needs to receive a multiplied blessing from distributing your paycheck. Show up early. Don't drop the ball on your assignments, keep a good attitude that builds important morale into others. You should be the MVP on any team – and your assist column should set records. *What do I need to do to make sure the team wins? Great, I'm on it.* That kind of thinking is counted as worship directed toward the King. He gets honored by your excellence. The boss will likely not have much reason to gripe if you keep this kind of posture. Work more hours than you're paid – on principle – invest more sweat and value than is common.

But let's say you do have a boss that is out to get you. You keep to it – keep your focus on honoring the King and building into people and bringing real value. That boss can write you up for everything under the sun, even fire you for no reason at all – and you will be able to walk away from your exit interview knowing you worked like the King's top-man every day. You did as instructed whether or not it was honored by your flesh-and-blood boss. If there is any doubt in your mind that you've been working for the King – that's an easy thing to fix. Repent. Reverse course and commit your ways to the Crown – declare to your wife and friends that you now see your employment differently than in the past. There won't be a regional pharmaceutical sales manager in the greater Ft. Lauderdale area that ever worked with as much gusto and joy as you, amigo! Let it rip. Your internal engine burns hot because you're powered by some serious juice – adoration for the King.

Subordinate roles can be tricky, no doubt, but learn from the good leaders and bad. Pay attention to what works, what keeps you motivated and empowered to climb to new heights because it's only a matter of time before you are given the command. You will be well suited for leadership because you operate in wisdom and have the King's nature pulsing through you. Lucky you! You know when to speak and when to keep your trap shut. You know how to address problems with patience and kindness while still demanding improvement and excellence. You have been with the King and so you reflect His nature. You're set up perfectly. Lacking something? Ask. The King gives to any Viceroy son who asks. Take a lowly stance and serve others – it will yield a good result.

AS AN ENTREPRENEUR

A Viceroy tells his story: *"You can be entrepreneurial. It's a risky move, no doubt about it. I went to a presentation last week where my brother (and business partner) spoke on a panel of entrepreneurs. Bright, young go-getters wrote notes as he spoke and I couldn't help but consider how expensive every one of his remarks and insights truly was. Every one of them cost us a mint, and these youngsters just gobbled them up for free! I sighed and then got over it! One of the quotes on the wall read: 'an entrepreneur is the kinda guy who jumps off a cliff and builds a plane on the way down.' It's very much exactly like that. No guarantees. Missed paychecks so you can make payroll for others. Lost sleep. Losing your cool with a partner who sees it all differently than you do. Broken partnership agreements. It's all a gigantic load of bliss with awesome-sauce drizzled over the top.*

"Sarcasm aside, it does offer a few perks. First, you get to build the culture you want to build. Second, there is freedom to

negotiate work hours and routines and family trips, etc. Third, you build something that passes down to others. Fourth, you get to personally invest your life in other people and see them mature and flourish (there are few things more rewarding than that!). Fifth, business is a blessing to clients. You build value into others every day you keep the shop open. It is one of the most optimistic and fruitful and faith-testing things a Viceroy can do; even so, there is no guarantee of success! You can face-plant and knock all your teeth out. That is a real possibility. Thrilling, no?!

"I am an extremely risk-averse person by nature. Since child-hood, I have always tried to pay attention and make good decisions. I missed out on a ton of fun, no doubt. Cautious to a fault, I never broke a bone and only once had two small stitches on a finger. There just isn't much 'rabble-rousing rowdiness' in me, so I was not a natural fit for the entrepreneurial life. Slow and steady, calm, and measured aren't the terms that come to mind with start-up life. And yet, almost nine years ago – the King told me to jump and start making an airplane. It was terrifying and I don't mean 'like a thrilling roller-coaster.' It felt more like 'a Russian-roulette kind of thrilling.' It was the last thing I wanted to do. Only now, years later, do I see that it was totally the right thing to do. The benefits of obedience to the King are rarely visible on the front-side of our 'yes' answer to the King. It just never seems to work that way."

In the pre-industrial age, the household was the epicenter of business. It's where the term 'cottage industry' comes from. All kinds of work happened in and around the home. A homestead was a multi-vertical kind of operation: farming, animal husbandry, smithing, making textiles, food production (churning butter), etc. all revolved around an industrious, multi-generational family trying to keep bellies fed and expand a little when the crops were especially good. The children were key to the household's success. They were homeschooled because they were home EVERYTHING-ed! They had a stake in the family's business and their training was critical for the future. Mom and Dad were not just titles, they were also labor bosses who kept the operation moving along.

Fast forward into the Industrial Age – and suddenly men, women, and children were scurrying all over cities into factories, offices, and school buildings. The father left the home only to return bedraggled and exhausted well after the sun dipped over the horizon. He was separated from his people for most of the day and slowly became the wage-earner absentee force that kept the roof in good repair and cars running. Post-WWII America took off and slowly the mother left the house as well to keep that double income dream alive and the standard of living still within reach.

We are at a unique moment in history that once again presents an exciting possibility. Viceroys can, thanks to the digital revolution, plausibly consider making a career that doesn't require total deployment away from the house. Side-hustles are converted into small business start-ups. The number of mothers who labor on-line and develop secondary, even tertiary income streams is staggering today. It may all feel like a scattered mishmash of entrepreneurial micro-movements – but keeping the lights on and bellies fed might have felt just as dangerous and fraught with tension in the pre-Industrial Era as it does today. You can begin to make micro-moves to become food-independent with an eye toward homesteading – Rory Groves did it – thegrovestead.com.

TWO INCOMES? (OR MORE!)

Wives hard at work in the home as children play at their feet? Sounds weird. Even idealistic, probably oppressive (barefoot and pregnant?) – depending on who you ask! A husband who works out of the home office and handles reading lessons between meetings? Welcome to the moment. All of it is possible, most of it is extremely difficult – but Viceroys who prioritize the house and Kingdom-culture enterprise are making it work hour by hour across the country.

When you hear **Proverbs 31** read aloud at church – well, at least the bits that are selected and placed on t-shirts – do you ever consider what is going on? Does it sound as shockingly and chaotically productive as it probably was? Start at the beginning of **Proverbs 31**. Verse one – these words came from King Lemuel's mother. We don't know who King Lemuel was – some have speculated that it is King Solomon, but the scholars don't agree. But don't just rocket off through that passage, stop and consider that opening; stop and consider that the instructions we read are the words of a woman, not just an average woman, a woman who raised a king. This is Viceroy-grade instruction here and it is why we read this passage over our wives at the weekly Sabbath/Shabbat meal. We affirm our wives that they are strong, beautiful, industrious, and kind.

A Viceroy guy testifies: *"Our family does a funny little thing when I recite Proverbs 31 over my wife. When I read the words 'from her profits' – the children say in unison 'Lord, bring profits!' and when I read 'her servants' the children say in unison, 'Lord, bring servants!' When we get to the end and I* say, 'Her children will rise up and say...' the children stand and recite the last couple of verses together: 'we call you blessed, for many daughters have done well, but you excel them all because charm is deceitful and beauty is vain, but a woman who fears the Lord shall be praised.'

"My wife is industrious. She learned it from her mother and grandmother and other saints who modeled a good example. She shows my children what Proverbs 31 looks like in the early days of this new century. She is the early riser and retires later in the evening. She tends to the needs of our household, those in need in our community, and other families in our neighborhood. She works from the home, but her work expands well outside our home; her reach and voice have exceeded all the boundaries we would have ever thought possible. She has been diligent (by necessity) because we've had to be inventive, resourceful, and dependent upon the King to make it rather than keep trading our hours and days for payment from a corporation or city government. "Entrepreneurship, while it blesses the entire household operation, also requires sacrifice from the entire household operation."

The **Proverbs 31** woman doesn't demand her place, she doesn't peacock for attention, she doesn't march and yell protest slogans to ensure she receives her justice, recognition, or expansion of rights. Yet she receives daily and weekly honor; her good example is hoisted up and applauded every week. Her faithfulness is celebrated. We want our wife to expand – to try new endeavors, to get more education, to start new companies. She's brilliant and we want her to reach her potential because as a daughter of the King, she will do many exploits in His name. We want the same for our daughters. **Proverbs 31** assumes multi-generational aristocratic wealth with servants. This woman has a support system in place.

So if the operations of our household are expanding, and if employees (servants) begin to multiply around us – our tents will expand. Those employees get a massive blessing as well. They get to see the King's people love, serve, create, and work as worship. They increase their skill sets, improve their resumes or portfolios, and broaden their vision of what a household can be in this modern moment. It feels archaic in one sense and yet it is refreshing, inspiring even because the King's table draws a crowd whenever it is set. This generation is earmarked by its depression, loneliness, isolation, and digital malaise. The King's table, *your* table as a Viceroy, nourishes the hungry and comforts the miserable. We have an opportunity to draw in those in need of the Kingdom. The King sets the lonely into families. That's your house! He's talking about your house and filling your table. If you have to pay people to work for you to purchase a voice in their life – do it! Drag people into your household and the warmth of your table will make a grand announcement that the King has a heart for your guests. The breaking of bread at your table will break open hearts.

BUILD INTO OTHERS (EMPLOYEES)

A final point: the term 'company' originates from the words for 'bread' *panem* in Latin. It literally means, 'those with whom I share my bread.' So you see, Viceroy operations exist for more than turning a profit and improving a balance sheet. It's about breaking bread, and our King is broken bread. That's where it starts getting fun – when the

King gets *more* honor. Occasionally, we get asked 'is your company a Christian company' and we generally smile and ask them to define their terms. We have employed all sorts of people, some aggressively hostile to the King's order, and we love it. We don't make people say their daily prayers or stop swearing or pass out Bibles. We want them to feel deeply loved and respected and 'built into' by our leadership team. We also think they are destined for the Kingdom.

We merely suggested 'entrepreneurship' in the paragraphs above. Let us lean even heavier on that point. If you are truly counterculture and you work for the average company, you're going to run into problems sooner or later with a boss, an HR department who looks at you with suspicion, or just the usual rough and tumble of downsizing and layoffs. Be developing a side-gig, side-hustle to see if the King doesn't bless you with a secondary option. Are you in pharmaceutical sales? Develop some unique proprietary tools for other salesmen. Draw from your experience and offer a consultation service? Take some of the extra income and get into real estate – a couple of investment properties. Do whatever it takes to diversify your employment. Remaining 'fully dependent' on an employer who is NOT loyal to you – no matter what the HR handbook says in the intro section – is unwise. Increasingly, corporate culture is NOT your friend. They don't like you and don't have your family's best interests in mind.

ON THE NEW FINANCIAL REALITIES (INFLATION/CHAOS ECONOMY/MODERN MONETARY THEORY)

We must be blunt here – there are forces moving against middle-class, faithful families in ways that are more often felt than perfectly identified or clearly articulated. We are increasingly falling into the economic reality put forward by the World Economic Forum, that: *in the future: you will own nothing and like it.* When you can only acquire extremely expensive housing (for purchase, not rent) at a high interest rate and it absorbs the lion's share of your monthly earnings, you are renting that property from the bank. IF you can maintain that – this enormous payment to the bank – you still face skyrocketing property taxes and this is a 'best case scenario' if you're a young married or young family man trying to jump up and catch that first rung on the property ladder. We know the previous generations did you no favors and our government seems most interested in helping the top earners stay at the top OR subsidizing the poor. Nobody is lying awake at night wondering how they can help a young pro like yourself afford a decent roof and brick walls and keep your wife at home to raise the babies. Don't count on that kind of assistance. True ownership of bigger assets seems more and more out of reach for the rising generations.

We have a hunch that the King's men are going to have to get very creative about how we make moves in the years ahead. We suspect that we're going to be FAR more invested (time and money) in helping get grandchildren up, educated, and maybe even housed – than our ancestors were. We can see church elders intentionally purchasing duplexes so that the young families in their churches can stay housed and then, perhaps, working a lease to own with owner financing to help them get an asset on their books. It will cost the older generations more, by necessity, to make heavier investments in the generations that follow us because the alternative is that the eager arms of the state will look entirely too inviting to the undiscerning and naïve. The moment demands creative vision.

But that brings us to the final point – the rising generations are going to have to light the old scripts on fire and begin anew. They aren't ready for this; it will shock many of them that it is normal AND GOOD for a man to work 60-75 hours a week. We are commanded to work six days and rest (totally rest) on the seventh. **Exodus 20:9-11:** *"Six days you shall labor, and do all your work, 10 but the seventh day is a Sabbath to the Lord your God. On it you shall not do any work, you, or your son, or your daughter, your male servant, or your female servant, or your livestock, or the sojourner who is within your gates. 11 For in six days the Lord made heaven and earth, the sea, and all that is in them, and rested on the seventh day. (ESV)"*

Ten to twelve-hour days are perfectly normal and okay for an ambitious man to work as he provides for his family. We know there's a big to-do about 'work-life balance' and 'self-care' – but Viceroys know that if it's going to pinch and be costly, then it should hit us first. We are willing to burn up the hours of our life in enterprise and the struggle against market-forces to see companies thrive. Who is going to cut all that hay? Do you intend to place that burden of provision upon your wife's shoulders? Your children? It's you, amigo. Get your mind right and get after it. Start the thing you've been thinking about, roll the lawnmower out of the garage and set up a shop. Start taking orders and fill them on your Saturday. Be up at 5 and crash at 10 – we are an anomaly on the timeline of history. Most of recorded history has been that of men doing hard (sometimes horribly nasty) jobs for an insane number of hours at meager pay. We have all kinds of advantages today and many of them (the tech, the systems) make our work easier. Force-multipliers and platforms and tools have come a very long way. It will still take a man of focused intensity, resolve, and (often) no other options to bring them to successful outcomes. You're that kind of man. You have a hard head, a soft heart, and thick skin. You are the man for the job and those under your care and good governance will thank you for it one day. So build your operations, amigo. We're pulling for you.

CHAPTER 9

RULING IN THE CHURCH

IT SHOULD BE the ambition of every Christian man to meet the qualifications of 'elder' in your local church. Whatever terms your particular church expression uses, the point remains: service to the Bride of Christ through governance is a particularly wonderful way to honor the King. His bride needs protection, direction, and care. Overseers. Pastors. Teachers. Deacons. The roles and responsibilities may vary, but make no mistake, male governance has never been in such short supply or more necessary than it is today.

Male headship is under constant assault and unrelenting ridicule. The result: the people suffer because of poor governance. St. Paul makes it rather plain: ruling elders and teachers of doctrine are to be men (**I Timothy 2:12**). You can dispute that the apostle meant it as plainly as that; you can consult other theological minds that make a case for women in church leadership. Many have. But these maneuvers will come at the expense of the flock entrusted to the care of men. It may also be true that your fellow churchmen wish to see women installed in these roles – we don't know where you assemble and worship. We can tell you this: St. Paul knew precisely what he was doing. Men protect the flock from wolves. Men are far more likely to stand on principle than soft-pedal for relational considerations. Men are simply better equipped to lock horns and fight like maniacs when the time comes for a real skirmish. Those flashpoint moments would wreck a woman; the relational turmoil and conflict load would cause her to waver rather than hold and make difficult or costly decisions.

For nearly 2,000 years, church governance was the exclusive responsibility of faithful, sacrificial men. Roughly 15 minutes ago, after the modern waves of feminism crashed against the cathedral doors, the cathedrals began closing or remodeling to rock-climbing gyms, as they have in Europe. We think there is a correlation here connecting feminism and the decline of the church in the West. Weakness. Apathy. Collusion with the world. All of these weakening forces are the result of emasculated men who gladly stepped back and away from their assigned responsibilities – from the Scripturally defined duties. We remain optimistic that churchmen are more awake, aware, and aggressive than in the past. We've seen too much. We know better now; we pray we know better now.

So, a young man should begin to position himself to serve the local church in whatever ways are available to him. Volunteer. Stay late and put up chairs and tables. Drop money in the offering plate as it goes by – faithfully tithe. Show up early to events and pitch in, drive the van to camp, and be present during prayer meetings. Begin the process of serving the Bride. In time, become a deacon, and then later – serve on a committee, or lead a mission trip, or organize a disaster relief trailer. There are so many ways that you can begin to cultivate a lifestyle of service. In time, as you become more 'elder-ly' – you may indeed meet the Biblical qualifications for church governance. 1 Timothy 3 describes deacons and shows how they serve their way into more leadership. Ruling a family well and showing wisdom in your job and temperance and hospitality in your local community, create the resume of a man who can be entrusted to govern the household of faith. That's the process; that's how it works.

The biggest hint here is that you need a very rare mindset shift. It is the practice of the day and the spirit of the age to be a CONSUMER. Americans are experts at consuming. The United States should be represented on all maps by a gigantic, gaping maw; we are the world's hungry mouth. We invented the 5-star Google review, the testimonial webpage, and the YouTube unboxing and product reviews. Consuming, you might say, is our national pastime. And tweeting mean things – we're also adept at tweeting sick burns. Consuming tendencies have so infiltrated our lives that we think of our church experiences the way we think of a dining experience. *The atmosphere was great. I liked the message, but the music was 'meh' and don't even get me started on the parking lot situation!*

We know of people who go to one service at one church for the opening worship segment and then drive 5 miles away to hear the preacher at another church. That is a consuming mindset. *What did I get out of that service? Did I feel delighted, satisfied, or encouraged?* This is a rotten way to consider your involvement in the local church; it is the most immature way to think of the assembly of the saints. By contrast, a mature man, a Viceroy, always begins with an INVESTING mindset. What value can we bring to this Sunday School class, to this prayer meeting, to this hospital visit? What can we do to help this church flourish? What unmet needs exist here? We just heard a guy say, *"Men won't do anything until they have to, but once they have to – men will do anything."* This is the primal, baseline wiring of all men. It's why it is far more difficult to be an invading or occupying force than it is to be a defensive force. It is difficult to motivate a man out of hatred for what stands in front of him, but he will bleed to death defending what stands behind him. The lives and well-being of his people and the city he loves motivate him; he would rather die than see his people and lands ravaged and pillaged.

This is the opposite of a consuming mindset – this is a total investment mindset. No sacrifice is too great if it means the flourishing and well-being of our people; this should be true of the elders of the local church. We can endure being called nasty names, hearing the lies among the whisperers, and having our character questioned. This rough treatment is just part of the larger duty to govern; it's the way we serve the Bride in service to the King. Very few men are willing to endure all that. Investor mindsets are rare, but they will be more necessary than ever as we move deeper into the 21st century.

Here is one last key point about the INVESTOR mindset – it always pushes resources down the generational line. Breathing one's last breath fat and happy in an expensive RV or golf course community is the last dying flare sent skyward by a consuming generation. Their last selfish hurrah!

A Viceroy throws in his story: *"I'll give you a story that* makes this point perfectly. A friend of mine told me the story of his church (it seems like it was in Florida?) that was full of rapidly aging parishioners. One year they discovered that the church had raised too much money because a dying older lady had activated her endowment. The church leadership put the matter of this surplus to a congregational vote: how would the church members like to see this money spent? All sorts of proposals flooded in – missions giving, food pantry, new baptismal installation, etc. When they got the input of the church members, they noticed two options had received the most interest and so they put it to a run-off vote.

"The first proposal came from the younger members – the families with young children. They asked for a daycare and early elementary school program with some facility modifications to accommodate the instruction of the children in their ABCs and the story of the boy with 5 loaves and 2 fish and John 3:16 and Moses'10 Commandments. The second proposal obviously came from the older members: they wanted on-site condominiums built, partially subsidized by the church so that the elderly could wind down their days among the friends they'd developed over the preceding decades. My friend simply could not believe that the result of the run-off vote was in favor of the condominiums rather than the small school. This is an egregious example of generational theft and the ultimate CONSUMER mindset. The older generation had no understanding of their chance to push resources into the rising generations. I hate to say it, but I see this played out very often in family storylines. Grandparents sip coffee on their multi-million dollar back porches, while their struggling children raise little ones on shoestring budgets. It ought not to be this way. The old make sacrifices that benefit the young; we always think of investment rather than consumption – this is a forgotten wisdom. Those who would govern the *church of tomorrow must keep this in mind. St. Paul wrote, 'Here for the third time I am ready to come to you. And I will not be a burden, for I seek not what is yours but you. For children are not obligated to save up for their parents, but parents for their children.* **2 Corinthians 12:14** *(ESV)'"*

The sad condition of the modern church is the result of a great many forces – evil forces, certainly, compounded by the simple erosion of virtue through a lack of wisdom. The older generations failed to impart, to hold fast to the doctrines of the apostles, to the veracity and wisdom of the Scriptures, and to male headship, exchanging it all for a post-enlightenment, modern liberal framework and the social respectability that it promised, with a grin. We implemented American business models and focused on branding and franchise campuses – and that required butts in seats and happy consumers.

We must re-discover our tenacity and resolve. We must straighten up again and rediscover our backbones. Christian men need their hands trained for war and we need to get our minds right: the Bride needs rescue, protection, and investment. Never cut deals. Never play footsies with the culture. Never bug out. You might just be the kind of guy willing to contend for others. You might be a guy ready to govern in the local church. Godspeed to you, sir. As you get down the road, turn around and train young men behind you – they probably won't know enough to ask for it, just grab them by the collar and tell them you both need a cup of coffee on Tuesday mornings.

CHAPTER 10
COMMUNITIES / CITY STREETS

THIS WILL BE a short chapter because the topic deserves its own treatment as a separate book title. We only want to emphasize that we are not navel-gazing introverts who shut out the larger world. We don't circle the wagons and cut ourselves off from a larger community – either the community of saints or our neighbors. Quiet pietism is not our posture; it can't be. We must engage. We must aim for more territory, and we reach outward. Dr. Stanley Hauerwas is quoted as saying, *"When other Christians tell me to retreat, to head for the hills, I always answer – retreat? hell, we're surrounded!"* He's right. There's nowhere to flee too – there is no 'new world' and we've run out of continent! Turn and fight and engage. Even so – everything has its season, and we can ask for Kingly wisdom. The bulk of the men who will hold this book in their hands and *actually read it* are primarily the 'under-forty' crowd. We know that. You sir, you young Christian man, you should have read enough at this point to be panting with your hands on your knees.

Your current life-stage should be exhausting; the

plowing and planting should mean you're collapsing into the bed at night with barely enough strength to offer sincere prayers with the wife. It is funny, however, that we do *somehow* manage to rise to the occasion if our romantic advances are welcomed – fatigue be damned! Er... moving on.

Those years before mid-life are packed to the brim with diligent labor for our employers (or jump-starting our own businesses), putting in garden boxes, comforting children with skinned knees, changing the brake pads, and keeping in close contact with other Viceroys striving to do the same. Beyond our families and our businesses, a Viceroy is connected to the King via his church – in some form or fashion. Attempting to 'viceroy' anything by your fleshly effort, brilliance or tenacity is a recipe for disaster. A deep connection to your spiritual community, submission to spiritual authorities, and routine examination by other men is paramount if you hope to endure in faithfulness to the King throughout your life.

So your spiritual community is non-negotiable. If you can't submit to others, don't kid yourself that you know how to submit to the King. It ain't gonna happen! Your rebel heart will betray you; your household will be a wreck. You risk becoming a tyrant, impulsive, demanding, and merciless or you'll swing to the other extreme as a passive, withdrawn, limp noodle of a man who keeps his fingers in his ears and wishes the shelling would stop. Don't get separated from your mission as a Viceroy because you get separated from your spiritual community. It happens all the time.

When you cross midfield – somewhere in your late forties, the expanse sort of 'opens up' and you get some margin back as the kids start heading off to college, or trade school, or the military. We are hesitant to put much weight (leadership responsibility) on young men who are juggling so much as they raise young families. While they prove their faithfulness in governing their homes, it opens up the possibility that these men may be leaders in the household of faith as they get space to serve in this capacity. The last thing we want is for young men with growing families to have to shoulder big community responsibilities that would subvert the King's culture they're building day by day in their households and business operations. But Viceroys do, in time, exercise their gifting and abilities in their faith communities. The qualifications of an elder, don't forget, require some sort of evidence that the man has managed his *own* household well. This is the great irony of today's congregations who have 28-year-old elders – in title only! Don't laugh – we've seen it.

Beyond the spiritual community, Viceroys are pretty certain that the King has plans for our streets and the *civitas* (oops, more Latin – *hey, what is this*?!), the larger community to which we belong. We have Viceroys involved in city-wide poverty initiatives, church pantry organizers who help street people eat a decent meal, tiny house village builders looking out for the homeless, school board servants, etc. Because we believe that the Kingdom must expand everywhere, from our hearts to our households and businesses and faith communities, then inevitably we will be caring about what happens on our streets. Viceroys roll up their sleeves and get to it.

More than likely, there are a great many initiatives already underway wherever you call home. When your family has the space to do so, participate as you can and let your kids know that "Hey, this town is our town. We care about what happens in our town. We don't like that people go hungry in our town. We can do something, even a little something, about that." That is a powerful message to a kid: we see a problem, we can get involved, and it helps at least this one person with a bag of groceries this week. Our King cared about 'the least of these' so we care about them, too. Make it a point to pray with them and ask the King for a blessing for your town and state – may the students in our city earn the highest test scores in the state, may our school campuses be safe and free from violence, give our city officials wisdom to know the best way to secure peace and order, keep our police officers safe, we pray for our two Senators in Washington, DC – may they be truthful and true to the people they represent, etc. May the true High King be honored in our nation. These kinds of prayers speak to a higher order in the chain of command – even the earthly powers are subject to our King.

If you know you are headed on an outing to a downtown area and you know you will probably be crossing paths with homeless or people asking for money – go ahead and fold up five or six dollar bills and keep them in your front pocket. Hand them out with a smile. Your kids will inevitably say, *"Geez Dad, you give them cash and you don't hand it out as easily to me when I ask!"* As they get older they will start asking questions about the ethical ramifications of helping fund a bad habit. All that is great discussion fodder for helping kids learn how they are to be Viceroys wherever they go. The generosity of our time and money speaks volumes to kids who know how precious both of those resources are – especially as we attempt to build so much.

A man who governs his heart, will gain authority over his life. This is a prerequisite for governing and handling the authority in one's home – with a wife and (hopefully) many children. From that position of authority, you'll likely find more responsibility and governing demands at work or in the company(s) you launch. A faithful and submitted man who governs his household well, is a great candidate to govern the household of faith – hold office in the church. See how all this works? The final domain that he can reach is whatever happens in his city, state, and nation – public life. Learning to govern well, to exercise dominion, takes decades and it's only then that you earn a place, a voice among the elders at the city gates. You can make civic decisions because you learned how and when to spank your toddler and create good policy around how you manage your two-car garage. It's a little-by-little transformation. You'd hate to have a city council manned by 19-year-old kids, or 24-year-old state senators. That's a recipe for disaster. Don't get us wrong, we're in favor of term limits and wish we didn't have octogenarians, 60 years in Washington DC, politicians. We don't prefer that, either!

Lastly, the nations. We're always amazed that the modern church sends its most insecure, untested, ill-equipped members to the mission fields. Think about it – college kids doing ministry tourism or young couples struggling with what it means to be married and young parents – *hey, let's send these poor souls because they seem to have energy and they are willing and fervent and have hearts to serve. Drop these young families into Surinam and let's pray they make it – in a hostile territory, in unfamiliar legal terrain, against regional principalities and forces they can't possibly imagine. They have a little Bible school training and a regional support person – they'll be fine!* We ought to be sending our seasoned veterans who've seen much and ministered well through periods of hardship and demonstrated long-obedience faithfulness. That's who we ought to send, if we were smart. 25-year marriages can handle so much more than three-year marriages and sending teams of seasoned couples would make the most sense of all. When we think of Viceroy training, we're certain that 'he that is faithful in a little, will be given much' – a promise that applies to other kinds (even international) of spiritual authority. So – learn to govern well, so you might govern much in the long run.

CHAPTER 11
'THE FUTURE BELONGS TO THE BRAVE'

A VICEROY TELLS HIS STORY: *"President Ronald Reagan said, 'the future doesn't belong to the fainthearted, it belongs to the brave.' He read his speech the very night that the Challenger space shuttle exploded on national television – America's children watched it happen real-time because there was a teacher on-board and there had been much excitement leading up to the launch. I know. I was in the school library watching it on the wheeled-in television set. Reagan was forced to console a nation and yet meet the national pain with stabilizing resolve and clench-jawed determination that we would again embark on space exploration. He chokes back his pain and tears in that broadcast and somehow rallies the public to endure sadness with resolve. Watch the clip online. He is a man who recognizes the moment in terms of the future. We grieve today and we should – it's fitting, he seems to be saying to the nation because we know we will go to the brink again tomorrow."*

So much of the Viceroy project that we undertake feels exactly this way. Daily we see our nation careening back and forth, bouncing into all the guardrails and wonder how it hasn't plunged to its total destruction. We have seen a great many Christian men and families self-immolate – infidelities, apostasies, addictions and collapse. As casualty reports roll in and we fight for others to stay the course, to hold the line, we are confronted with the possibility of despair. We cannot quit the field because everything and everyone we love is at stake. In many ways, as men, we are the Divinely constructed instrument, uniquely formed, to be able to comfort the downtrodden while fixing bayonets for yet another advance when commanded. We wonder how we will ever keep the family finances in the black when we are playing such long-game investments in the things not measured on spreadsheets.

This is no minor feat. This is not a boy's errand. The longer we stand, the greater the chance others have to see breakthroughs. There's a maxim attributed to General Patton – *never bleed for the same ground twice.* That's a fantastic line. The victories gained in this generation of my family line should be chronicled and recited and imparted so the next generation doesn't have to bleed for my acreage again. They will bleed for theirs.

Our King made a promise that masquerades as a command in **Matthew 6**. *"But seek first the kingdom of God and His righteousness, and all these things shall be added to you."* We often think of this verse as a 'thou shalt' styled command and it is, but it is also an invitation into obedience that secures our basic provision. Food, drink, clothing – the necessities of our households are covered when we submit to the King's governance. We don't worry about the future – today's fight is fight enough. Today's victory is assured because our King doesn't lose – we walk as closely as we can to Him because his record is *total victory all the time*. Separating myself from the King and His interests will assure the collapse of most of what comprises my life; it's that simple.

Viceroys walk in optimism when we consider the horizon before us – because the King is on our horizon; He is in our future no matter what that future holds. He will be King when our grandsons are in their fight. We're greatly encouraged because we see men waking up from their strange stupor. Remember in our introduction when Gordon Dalby made his concerns known about men only receiving their identity from their work and doom-scrolling on their smartphones? This generation of men is waking up to the fragility of such thinking. We see a world where our careers won't culminate in a retirement party after 35 years with the company. The world, the economy, the trends just don't work that way anymore. Young men are becoming acutely aware that trading one's life for mere money or prestige or security is a hollow exchange. We see it every day – young men are asking these fundamental questions more often and with greater fervor than they ever have. Dalby lamented our fascination with our screens that suck our lives by the hour – a drip-feed of anesthesia for men who don't want to feel their pain. We see more men finally talking about their 'porn portal in their pocket' than we ever have. Men are talking about and getting angry with what we see around us, and we are submitting to the King as never before.

Obedience produces more obedience. Discipline creates more space for greater discipline. Somehow, when we get our finances in order, we eat better, and when that is tacked down, we exercise more, and that creates better rest and enjoyment of our family. Obedience and discipline as a man under command, a man under the King, creates more freedom. Truly righteousness yields the peace and joy we sought through our own stupidity and half-hearted efforts. A repenting and yielding knee in the dirt opens up possibilities we could never have seen. We want more of His order and nearness the more territory He governs. He is after all of it. He wants that back 90-acre parcel that doesn't drain well – He wants our swampland heart drained and put under production. We do, too. God help us.

Many of the men in our local Viceroy chapter are crossing into new territory in the next ten years: children married off and grandkids screaming their little heads off. Some of us will be approaching 'retirement age' with absolutely NO interest in retiring. What a bizarre and unbiblical concept! We hope to see more employees popping to new life with new purpose, skills, and prosperity in our companies. Then we hope to see them build it into others and enlarge their own tents. We can't think of anything better. We hope to see our networked community of men grow and spread out across the globe. We need to know other men in Virginia Beach or London or Boston who are specialists in certain businesses, who have special insight into the King's ambition. We want to do business with men who, like us, wish to push blessing into the earth. We will send our children to work under your tutelage. You can send yours to Texas. The King's culture is global, and advancing; the King's men properly allied, encouraged, equipped together will move from victory to victory. With God, we will do valiantly. (**Psalm 60:12**) You are most welcome to join us.

You Are the Fight.

BOOKS MENTIONED OR RECOMMENDED

- *Healing the Masculine Soul* – Gordon Dalbey
- *Man of the House* – C.R. Wiley
- *The Household and the War for the Cosmos* – C.R. Wiley
- *Ploductivity: A Practical Theology of Work and Wealth* – Doug Wilson
- *Becoming a King* – Morgan Snyder
- *Oikonomics* – Mike Breen
- *Fathered By God* – John Eldridge
- *The Benedict Option* – Rod Dreher
- *Durable Trades* – Rory Groves
- *The Family Economy* – Rory Groves
- *Masculine Christianity* – Zachary Garris
- *No Apologies* – Anthony Esolen
- *Full-Time* – David Bahnsen
- *Leadership and Emotional Sabotage* – Joe Rigney

A NOTE ON SUBMISSION

A bit more clarity on Submission: in the New Testament, the English term *submit* is[1] *hypotasso* (Strong's # G5293) which is translated "be subject to" and "to submit to" in the ESV and NASB.[2] The meaning in the Greek is: to arrange under, to subject, etc. It is a Greek military term meaning "to arrange [troop divisions] in a military fashion under the command of a leader." In non-military use, it was a "voluntary attitude of giving in, cooperating, assuming responsibility, and carrying a burden."

Jesus submitted to his earthly parents (Lk 2:51), we are told to submit to authorities (Rom 13:1,5, Tit 3:1, 1Pe 2:13), women submit to their husbands (1Co 14:34, Col 3:18, Tit 2:5, 1Pe 3:1,5), slaves submit to their masters (Tit 2:9, 1Pe

---

1. Interestingly, the only exception is Hebrews 13:17, where we are told to submit to church leadership. This term is *hypeiko* (Strong's # G5226) which means to: resist no longer, but to give way, yield (as of combatants). So this is a very different concept.
2. In the KJV (and perhaps other older translations) a few times (incorrectly): "to be obedient to" or "to subdue". This gives entirely the wrong idea.

2:18), young men submit to elders (1Pe 5:5), the Church (Eph 5:24) and all things will submit to Jesus (1Co 15:28, Eph 1:22, Php 3:21, Heb 2:5,8, 1Pe 3:22), and finally, we are to submit to God (Jas 4:7). There are a few other similar, or metaphorical uses along these same lines. All with the same meaning of being in an orderly manner under the authority of another.

So much for the usage and meaning. But a few interesting things to point out. First, the person submitting is not lesser in value and not necessarily lesser in status, ability or any other human measure. In 1Co 16:15-16 Paul commands his readers to submit to "every fellow worker and laborer." And the first usage of this term is when Jesus submits to his own parents, who he had created. Second, to submit is not the same as to obey. When most people read "submit" they think in these terms, and they are somewhat connected, but these terms do not carry the same idea. Children are told to obey their parents (Eph 6:1, Col 3:20) and slaves their masters (Eph 6:5, Col 3:22) but wives are never told to obey their husbands![3]

Putting all of this together, submission in the New Testament is commanded of all of us. Each is to submit to those in authority over him or her. This command does not imply that there is a difference in value, ability, or even experience or intelligence or wisdom. Rather, it is about proper order that God has set in place. The military roots of this term bring these things to light. Very often soldiers are vastly stronger and more powerful, more skilled, and

---

3. Some translations might say "obey" but not the good ones, which are consistent in how they translate this term. 1Pe 3:1 it says wives should *submit* to their husbands, even those who do not *obey* the Word.

often more experienced, than their commanding officers. Many of these grizzled old warriors have skills and abilities their generals couldn't even describe, much less carry out. And yet, these soldiers put themselves unquestioningly in submission to their commanding officer. They use all the experience, training, skill, and wisdom at their disposal, to carry out the goals of their commanding officer. They understand that their commanding officer is also under authority.

In military mission planning, there is a document called the *Commander's Intent*. It could be defined as: "A broad description and definition of what a successful mission will look like in its end state. It is the single unifying focus for all subordinate elements, so it must be understood by the echelons below the commander. Commander's intent helps communicate the vision clearly. It describes what success looks like to all members."[4] So, before a mission, each soldier needs to understand the end goal by reading this 1-page document. With this in mind, we can understand a major difference between obeying and submitting. A soldier must obey his orders UNLESS they go against the Commander's Intent that he is in submission to. So, if his commanding officer gives him a command that is contrary to the goal, he knows that he should not obey it. And if his commanding officer gives him an order that he is in the midst of carrying out, he must still use his best judgement in order to accomplish the ultimate goals. Imagine a scenario where the Commander's Intent specifies that the ultimate goal of the mission

4. https://pavilion.dinfos.edu/Article/Article/2163950/the-elements-of-commanders-intent/

is the capture of the enemy general. A certain soldier is obeying his orders by fighting in a specific place, but then spies the enemy general making a getaway, his submission to the ultimate goal might require him to disobey a direct order, and turn and give chase to the enemy general. So he would be submitting, not blindly obeying what he is told.

In summary, submission is about ordering yourself under your authority, learning his or her ultimate goals, and then using all of your skills and abilities, knowledge and wisdom, experience, and strength to accomplish those goals. It is not about doing your own will until you are told to do something by the person over you in authority, and then begrudgingly obeying. Not at all, it is about putting yourself wholeheartedly in submission and making their goals, your goals. A slave or a child is told to obey whether he understands what he is doing or not, whether he agrees with it, and whether it is against his own goals. But a wife is not told to obey, she is told to submit. She is to be one with her husband, and that includes his goals and purpose. We are to obey God, to obey the commands, whether we like to or not. But James, the brother of Jesus, gives us the higher command. Submit to God. Submission is what makes obedience easier.

VICEROY

www.ingramcontent.com/pod-product-compliance
Lightning Source LLC
Chambersburg PA
CBHW071719140626
46557CB00012B/967